SOCIAL STRATIFICATION IN POLAND

Eight Empirical Studies

Edited with an introduction by
Kazimierz M. Słomczyński
and Tadeusz K. Krauze
With a foreword by Gerhard Lenski

Routledge
Taylor & Francis Group

LONDON AND NEW YORK

First published 1986 by M.E. Sharpe

Reissued 2018 by Routledge
2 Park Square, Milton Park, Abingdon, Oxon OX14 4RN
711 Third Avenue, New York, NY 10017, USA

Routledge is an imprint of the Taylor & Francis Group, an informa business

Copyright © 1986 by Taylor & Francis

Published simultaneously as vol. xvi, no. 1-2 of *International Journal of Sociology*.

Translated by Ray Taras

No part of this book may be reprinted or reproduced or utilised in any form or by any electronic, mechanical, or other means, now known or hereafter invented, including photocopying and recording, or in any information storage or retrieval system, without permission in writing from the publishers.

Notices
No responsibility is assumed by the publisher for any injury and/or damage to persons or property as a matter of products liability, negligence or otherwise, or from any use of operation of any methods, products, instructions or ideas contained in the material herein.

Practitioners and researchers must always rely on their own experience and knowledge in evaluating and using any information, methods, compounds, or experiments described herein. In using such information or methods they should be mindful of their own safety and the safety of others, including parties for whom they have a professional responsibility.

Product or corporate names may be trademarks or registered trademarks, and are used only for identification and explanation without intent to infringe.

Publisher's Note
The publisher has gone to great lengths to ensure the quality of this reprint but points out that some imperfections in the original copies may be apparent.

Disclaimer
The publisher has made every effort to trace copyright holders and welcomes correspondence from those they have been unable to contact.

A Library of Congress record exists under LC control number: 85018387

ISBN 13: 978-1-138-03760-1 (hbk)
ISBN 13: 978-1-138-03764-9 (pbk)
ISBN 13: 978-1-315-17781-6 (ebk)

SOCIAL STRATIFICATION IN POLAND

Eight Empirical Studies

Table of Contents

Acknowledgments vii

Foreword
GERHARD LENSKI ix

Introduction: The Background of Recent Polish Research on Social Stratification
KAZIMIERZ M. SŁOMCZYŃSKI
and TADEUSZ K. KRAUZE 3

Social Inequality and Social Mobility
MICHAŁ POHOSKI 30

Changes in Social Structure and in How It Is Popularly Perceived
KRYSTYNA JANICKA 60

The Attainment of Occupational Status: A Model with Multiple Indicator Constructs
KAZIMIERZ M. SŁOMCZYŃSKI 78

Dichotomous Class Images and Worker Radicalism
WOJCIECH ZABOROWSKI 105

The Subjective Evaluation of Social Status
KAZIMIERZ M. SŁOMCZYŃSKI
and GRAŻYNA KACPROWICZ 124

The Prestige of Education
ZBIGNIEW SAWIŃSKI   144

Value Systems among Occupational Groups
MARIA MISZTAL   160

Social Mobility: Actual,
Perceived, and Equitable
TADEUSZ K. KRAUZE and
KAZIMIERZ M. SŁOMCZYŃSKI   174

About the Authors   191

Acknowledgments

The editors thank the Institute of Sociology of the University of Warsaw for providing a leave to Kazimierz M. Słomczyński which enabled him to work on this volume. They are also grateful to the Institute of Philosophy and Sociology of the Polish Academy of Sciences for being a host to Tadeusz K. Krauze during his several visits to Warsaw, to Hofstra University for partially releasing him from teaching obligations, and to the International Research and Exchanges Board (IREX) for providing him with travel grants. Jerzyna Słomczyńska and Robin Krauze are thanked for continuous aid in the preparation of this volume.

K.M.S. and T.K.K.

Foreword

In recent years, the American press and American television news have been filled with stories from Gdańsk, Warsaw, Kraków, Łódź, and other Polish cities and towns. During this period, the names of a number of Polish leaders have become almost as familiar to Americans as the names of their own leaders, and the word "Solidarity" has acquired an important new meaning for Americans as well as Poles.

Unfortunately, however, this interest of the American public has not been matched by corresponding interest from American sociologists. Polish society is seldom mentioned either in our major scholarly journals or in the textbooks written for our students.

This lack of interest in Polish society on the part of American sociologists reflects, of course, the general disinterest in societies other than our own. As Everett Hughes (1961) observed nearly a quarter of a century ago, American sociology has become an "ethnocentric sociology." It has lost its enthusiasm for the kind of comparative analysis that was central to the work of the founders of the discipline and that gave substance to their writings.

The neglect of Polish society is especially unfortunate at the present time, since Poland is part of the socialist bloc of societies and has, since the end of World War II, been a testing ground for numerous ideas derived from Marxist theory. In view of the growing tendency of American sociologists to regard Marx as one of the founders and most important and innovative theorists of our discipline, one might suppose that this would ensure a lively interest in socialist societies, especially one in which sociological research is as vigorous as it is in Poland.

Poland has a long and rich tradition of sociological research and writing dating back to the nineteenth century. This tradition was interrupted briefly during the German occupation in World War II and in the early years following the establishment of the present Marxist regime. But as early as 1956, restrictions began to be lifted and sociological research and writing were able to resume.

Viewed from an American perspective, this new era of Polish sociology has been remarkable for its vitality, and also for its intellectual independence, objectivity, and freedom from ideological cant. In all these respects, the contrast between Polish sociology and Soviet sociology has been quite remarkable. While much of the credit for this is obviously due to political differences between the two societies, some of the credit is also due to the leadership provided by a number of key individuals, such as Stanisław Ossowski, Jan Szczepański, Stefan Nowak, and Włodzimierz Wesołowski.

As Słomczyński and Krauze explain in their introduction to this volume, since 1964 the Institute of Philosophy and Sociology of the Polish Academy of Sciences has sponsored, under the leadership of Wesołowski, a series of large-scale research projects dealing with questions of stratification and inequality. This is both an important subject and a sensitive one in socialist societies, since the findings of projects such as these have political, as well as scholarly implications.

Students of stratification everywhere will be forever indebted to the men and women who have created the now substantial store of information concerning inequality and its consequences in a socialist society. Their work provides us with a rich body of data that we, as well as they, can use to test some of the most important ideas in our discipline.

Polish sociology is also important because geographical and historical circumstances have forced Polish sociologists to wrestle with basic questions of theory and method to a much greater degree than many of the rest of us. In particular, they have been forced by circumstances to deal with the contradictions within and between the Marxist and the functionalist traditions. In the process, they seem to have created, or to be in process of creating, a novel synthesis of their own—yet one that can prove of benefit to sociologists everywhere. Thanks to their publications, those of us who have not shared their experiences are still able to benefit from them.

Fortunately for American sociologists, much of modern Polish sociology is available in English. At an early date, our Polish colleagues recognized the importance of translation and established the *Polish Sociological Bulletin*, a journal that has published translations of important papers in English for more than twenty years. In addition, many other interesting papers and monographs have been made available in translation. Some of them have been published in Poland (e.g., Allardt and Wesołowski, 1978), while others have been published abroad (e.g., Staniszkis, 1983, or Słomczyński and Krauze, 1978). The present volume is a good example of this tradition, and provides a rich and valuable sample of contempory research in the field of stratification.

Thanks to studies such as those published here and numerous others like them by other Eastern European sociologists, the basis now exists for developing a sociology of socialist industrial societies. No longer is it necessary to think of socialism merely as an abstract set of ideals or as a mysterious *terra incognita*. Although it is true that certain very important aspects of life in even the most open of socialist societies still remain off-limits to researchers, the same is true to some degree of all societies. What is more important is that we now have more than enough data to develop meaningful models of socialist industrial societies and of the forces shaping their development (see, for example, Jones, 1983). For this, we are all greatly indebted to the daring, innovative, and imaginative Polish sociologists who pioneered in the study of socialist systems of stratification in the late 1950s and to those who have joined them more recently, carrying on the tradition while substantially expanding our knowledge and understanding of these systems.

Gerhard Lenski
Chapel Hill, North Carolina
March 1985

References

Allardt, E. and W. Wesołowski (eds.)
    1978   *Social Structure and Change: Finland and Poland in Comparative Perspective.* Warsaw: Polish Scientific Publishers.

Hughes, E.
    1961   "Ethnocentric Sociology." *Social Forces* 40:1-4.

Jones, T. A.
    1983   "Models of Socialist Development." *International Journal of Comparative Sociology* 24:86-99.

Słomczyński, K. M. and T. Krauze (eds.)
    1978   *Class Stucture and Social Mobility in Poland.* White Plains, N.Y.: M. E. Sharpe.

Staniszkis, J.
    1983   *Poland's Self-Limiting Revolution.* Princeton: Princeton University Press.

Social Stratification in Poland

Eight Empirical Studies

Introduction

The Background of Recent Polish Research on Social Stratification

KAZIMIERZ M. SŁOMCZYŃSKI
and TADEUSZ K. KRAUZE

This volume can be considered a sequel to *Class Structure and Social Mobility in Poland* (Słomczyński and Krauze, 1978), published seven years ago. In the intervening period there has been a great deal of turbulence in Poland: a political and economic crisis, resulting in the establishment of the Solidarity labor movement in 1980; the crackdown on Solidarity and the imposition of martial law in 1981; then the lifting of martial law and the proclamation of an amnesty in July 1983, with gradual stabilization and a reimposition of party control since that time. Throughout this period sociologists in Poland have been observing, analyzing, and interpreting the changing situation, while striving to conduct empirical research and publish their results. Some examples of this work are collected here.

Our intention in this introduction is to sketch the theoretical and empirical background of the papers that follow. We begin with a discussion of the research tradition and organizational context of social stratification studies in Poland. Then we review the most relevant studies on the three major research topics represented in this volume: inequality among occupational groups, social mobility, and psychological aspects of social stratification. Some bibliographical information is provided at the end of the essay.

The research context

The theoretical point of departure for much of the empirical research on stratification in Poland is Stanisław Ossowski's classic work, *Class Structure in the Social Consciousness* (1957; English translation 1963). Its importance stems from the successful synthesis Ossowski carried out on two levels: a comparison of the Marxist and functionalist views of class structure and social stratification, and a comparison of social inequality in capitalist and socialist systems. Although Ossowski's work was primarily theoretical, his elaboration of concepts and the relationships among various features of social structures serves to this day as an inspiration for Polish sociologists engaged in empirical research. Ossowski's moral and scholarly authority also rests upon numerous contributions that are not available in English. After his death in 1964, a Polish edition of his collected works was published in six volumes.

An explicitly Marxist program of theoretical and empirical research on the working class was outlined in the mid-1950s by Hochfeld (1956). This program was implemented and extended by Szczepański, who was concerned with the historical roots of the Polish working class and intelligentsia. Szczepański's research was popularized in his book, *Polish Society* (1970; see also 1978).

Since 1964, the Institute of Philosophy and Sociology of the Polish Academy of Sciences has sponsored large-scale research projects devoted to the investigation of class structure and stratification. These projects became institutionalized in a program included in a governmental research plan for the social sciences. This program, directed by Włodzimierz Wesołowski until 1981, generated further problems for investigation and provided full-time work for many sociologists. Adequate financial support was assured, research output was steady (in terms of books alone, more than twenty volumes were produced), and many young sociologists wrote their Ph.D. dissertations on the basis of the data collected. Work connected with this program comprises the mainstream of Polish studies on social stratification.

During the 1970s three major theoretical propositions guided empirical research in Poland. First, it was assumed that the socialist transformation of the economic system would gradually diminish the role of the Marxian criterion of class position—that is, the property of the means of production—and enhance the autonomous role of such attributes as education, authority and power, income and standard of living, cultural participation, and prestige. Accordingly, studies focused on the decreasing importance of social differences among the three major social classes—the intelligentsia, the working class, and the peasantry. Second, it was assumed that the division of labor, resulting in occupational differentiation, would become the central mechanism for the structuring of society. Studies were therefore conducted on the distribution of desired goods and values among occupational groups. Third, it was assumed that, for individuals as units of analysis, the relationship among basic status characteristics such as education, authority, income, and prestige would weaken over time, as a consequence of state policies. Thus much research was devoted to status inconsistency and its psychological effects—not only the negative effects (e.g., reactions to stress or the feeling of deprivation), but positive ones as well (e.g., belief in the new rules of social justice or satisfaction derived from compensating rewards). Much of the research based on these three guiding propositions is reviewed by Wesołowski and Słomczyński (1977); see also the papers collected in Słomczyński and Krauze (1978) and the Polish Sociological Association (1978).

To a significant degree the research program outlined above integrated functional concepts, terminology, and research topics into a Marxist framework. Analyses of Marx's theory of social structure (e.g., Hochfeld, 1963, 1967; Wesołowski, 1967; Jasińska and Nowak, 1973; Kozyr-Kowalski, 1970) and its implications for studying socialist society (e.g., Wesołowski, 1969; Ładosz, 1977; Widerszpil, 1978; Drążkiewicz, 1980; Hryniewicz, 1983) influenced research practice to a lesser extent than might have been expected in a country with a long Marxist sociological tradition.

The political events of the 1980s have led to a change in Polish sociologists' theoretical perspective on class structure and social stratification. The change is manifested in a greater focusing on social conflict, including the formation and articulation of group interests. Thus, the relatively dormant conflict-theory aspects of Marxist sociology have revived and gained in importance. Parallel to this development, some fragmentation of the previously consolidated program of research has occurred, allowing for the application of innovative methodological approaches based on humanistic sociology. It is perhaps too early for a balanced assessment of the permanent value of these contributions.

Both theoretically and methodologically, the papers in this volume continue the presented mainstream tradition of the mainstream of Polish research on social stratification. They investigate the classical research problems: inequality among occupational groups (Pohoski, Janicka), intergenerational occupational mobility (Słomczyński, Pohoski), perception of social structure (Zaborowski, Janicka), and other psychological aspects of social stratification (Słomczyński and Kacprowicz, Sawiński, Misztal). The papers were commissioned by the editors in 1982. With the exception of Krauze and Słomczyński's paper, all of them are based on data collected prior to or during 1980; however, the ways the data have been interpreted reflect a shift in theoretical interest. Concern with social conflict is particularly evident in the papers of Janicka, Pohoski, and Zaborowski.

Inequality among occupational groups

All of the papers contained in this volume regard occupational differentiation as the basis for the unequal distribution of socially desirable goods and values. Accordingly, the fundamental variable, occupation, requires close examination.

Polish dictionaries of occupational titles, constructed for census purposes, contain sixteen to twenty thousand items. The sociological problem consists in constructing a classification of a manageable number (up to three hundred) of narrow occupational categories which are exhaustive, mutually exclusive, and homogeneous with respect to type of work. This classification should be amenable to aggregation to a still smaller number (up to twenty) of large occupational groups.

Three classifications have been proposed. Zagórski (1971) adjusted the classification used in the decennial census. Wesołowski created a scheme (1970) that was used for surveys in urban areas. Another classification, developed by Pohoski et al. (1974), was modified by Pohoski and Słomczyński (1978). This last classification, known as the Social Classification of Occupations, was recommended by the Polish Academy of Sciences for use in all research on social stratification in Poland. It also served as the basis for constructing occupational scales according to complexity of work, socioeconomic status, and prestige. The work of Słomczyński and Kacprowicz (1979) contains the values of three scales for all narrowly defined occupational categories and their various aggregations.

Ten large occupational groups were established by the Social Classification of Occupations (see Table 1). The criteria for distinguishing these groups are as follows: relationship to the means of production, manual versus nonmanual work, type of enterprise in which the work is performed, level of occupational skill required, and production versus service type of work. Domański (1983) investigated the homegeneity of each occupational group with respect to such sociologically significant characteristics of occupations as average education, average income, level of position with respect to decision making (i.e., power), and prestige. The aim of Domański's analysis was to predict the percentage of occupations that would be correctly assigned to each group only on the basis of these four social characteristics. Using multivariate nominal analysis, he predicted the percentages presented in the last column of Table 1.

The Social Classification of Occupations was not explicitly based on any of the four variables taken into consideration by Domański. His results show that the occupational groups of managers, professionals, technicians, skilled workers, semi-skilled and unskilled workers, and entrepreneurs are relatively homo-

Table 1

Major Occupational Groups, Number of Occupational Categories Included in these Groups, and the Proportion of Occupational Categories Correctly Classified on the Basis of Four Variables: Education, Income, Power, and Prestige[a]

Major occupational groups	Number of occupational categories	Proportion of occupational categories correctly classified
Managers	39	.82
Professionals	60	.80
Technicians	43	.79
Office workers	21	.29
Service workers	25	.64
Skilled workers	67	.76
Unskilled workers	48	.85
Farmers	5	.00
Entrepreneurs	11	1.00
Others	10	.00
Total	329	.73

[a]Based on Domański, 1983: Tables 2 and 3.

geneous: more than 75 percent of their respective occupations would be included in those groups on the basis of education, income, power, and prestige.

In studies of the relationship among occupation, education, and income, the typical units of analysis are individuals. Table 2 summarizes the results of three studies in which a correlation for each pair of variables was computed. It can be seen that the relationship between education and occupation is stronger than the one between education and income or the one between occupation and income. In addition, the strength of these correlations is stable through time.

Social mobility

Recently Goyder (1984) compared two approaches to the study of

Table 2

Correlations among Education, Occupation, and Income for the Economically Active Population in Poland, 1972-78

Sample	Education and occupation	Education and income	Occupation and income
Males and females, aged 30 to 39, 1972 N = 13,000[a]	.48	.32	n.a.
Males and females, aged 18 to 65, 1975 N = 3,574[b]	.42	.32	.33
Males, aged 19 to 65, 1978 N = 1,557[c]	.51	.27	.32

[a]Pohoski et al., 1978: Table 7.
[b]Alestalo et al., 1978: Table 3.
[c]Based on data from Słomczyński et al., 1981.

social mobility: the categorical analysis of the mobility table and the regression analysis of status attainment. These two approaches, dominant in the literature on social mobility, should be seen as complementary rather than alternative. Both are represented in this volume: Pohoski applies categorical analysis and Słomczyński uses regression analysis.

Analysis of mobility tables

The link between the categorical analysis of the mobility table and the regression analysis of status attainment is provided by canonical correlation analysis (Klatzky and Hodge, 1971). Domański and Sawiński (1984) computed the canonical correlation between the statuses of fathers and sons for 1982 data from a national random sample of men over eighteen years of age. Their result (.495) falls between the values for the United States (.423) and

Australia (.525) as reported by Featherman *et al.* (1975). Domański and Sawiński also show that the socioeconomic dimension captures the social-mobility process better than the pure prestige dimension. This finding is consistent with the results for the United States.

The predominant mode of analysis of the mobility table is based on multiplicative models originated by Goodman (1969) and Hauser (1978). In this volume Pohoski's work utilizes Hauser's approach of multi-level modeling of the mobility table. The structure of Pohoski's model is similar to one applied in the comparison of mobility processes in England, Sweden, and France (Erikson *et al.*, 1982).

An alternative approach, focusing on circulation and structural mobility, was proposed by Krauze and Słomczyński (1986). They defined structural mobility as the part of total mobility that preserves the difference between origin and destination distributions, and minimizes the total number of status transitions. Circulation mobility is conceived as the part of total mobility, in which the origin and destination distributions are equal and the total number of status transitions is maximized. Matrix representations of circulation mobility and structural mobility have nonnegative values and add up to the table of total observed mobility. The technique of linear programming was used to find the transition frequencies in these matrices.

Pohoski's data on the social mobility of men, ages 30-39, were collected in 1972. There is another set of data on the mobility of Polish men, ages 18 and over ($N = 36,503$), from the same year. These data are presented in Table 3, together with the most recent data, for a strictly comparable national sample surveyed in 1982. This table also provides the frequencies of circulation mobility; matrices of immobility and structural mobility can be obtained by subtracting the circulation mobility matrix from the matrix of total mobility.

Generally, the patterns of both total and circulation mobility are similar for 1972 and 1982. The amount of total mobility is almost the same for both years (about 45 percent), while circula-

Table 3

Total and Circulation Mobility from Father's Occupation to Son's Current Occupation for Men over 18 Years of Age, in 1972 and 1982; with Sample Sizes Standardized to 10,000[a]

Father's occupation	Son's occupation				
	White collar	Blue collar	Petite bourgeoisie	Farmer	Total
	1972[b]				
White collar	519 (0)	336 (336)	12 (12)	11 (11)	878 (359)
Blue collar	750 (359)	2,599 (0)	49 (49)	198 (198)	3,596 (606)
Petite bourgeoisie	82 (0)	146 (97)	32 (0)	31 (31)	291 (128)
Farmer	627 (0)	2,162 (173)	67 (67)	2,379 (0)	5,235 (240)
Total	1,978 (359)	5,243 (606)	160 (128)	2,619 (240)	10,000 (1,333)
	1982[c]				
White collar	767 (0)	526 (526)	44 (44)	38 (38)	1,375 (608)
Blue collar	849 (580)	2,705 (0)	99 (99)	219 (219)	3,872 (898)
Petite bourgeoisie	82 (28)	99 (99)	22 (0)	16 (16)	219 (143)
Farmer	570 (0)	2,004 (273)	71 (0)	1,889 (0)	4,534 (273)
Total	2,268 (608)	5,334 (898)	236 (143)	2,162 (273)	10,000 (1,922)

[a] Values of circulation mobility given in parentheses.
[b] Zagórski, 1976:186.
[c] Based on data reported in Domański and Sawiński, 1984:120.

tion mobility increased slightly (from 13 to 19 percent). In Table 4 the proportions of circulation and structural mobility are given for transitions from father's occupation to son's occupation at two time points—first job and current job. Between 1972 and 1982 the decrease in the amount of structural mobility is negligible in the case of transition to first occupation, and small in the

Table 4

The Proportion of Total Intergenerational Mobility, Structural Mobility, Circulation Mobility, and Immobility for Men over 18 Years of Age, in 1972 and 1982[a]

Types of mobility	From father's occupation to son's first occupation		From father's occupation to son's current occupation	
	1972	1982	1972	1982
Total mobility	.3995	.4416	.4471	.4617
structural mobility	.2780	.2752	.3138	.2695
circulation mobility	.1215	.1664	.1333	.1922
Immobility	.6005	.5584	.5529	.5383
Total	1.0000	1.0000	1.0000	1.0000

[a]Source as in Table 3.

case of transition to current occupation. These results cast doubt on arguments that the relatively high amount of total mobility is attributable to structural mobility, forced by changes between origin and destination distributions (Connor, 1979; Andorka and Zagórski, 1980).

Status attainment

Słomczyński's paper demonstrates that, among the determinants of occupational status, education plays a predominant role. The same result has been reported in other studies. For example, Figure 1, constructed on the basis of data from Pohoski et al. (1978), shows that the explanatory power of education with respect to occupational status is relatively high. Therefore, the determinants of education should be studied in their own right.

Białecki (1982) provides data on educational selection in major social classes. Using national statistics on the class origin of students who graduated from elementary schools in 1970, Białecki presented the sequential process of attrition at more advanced levels of schooling. Table 5 describes the educational

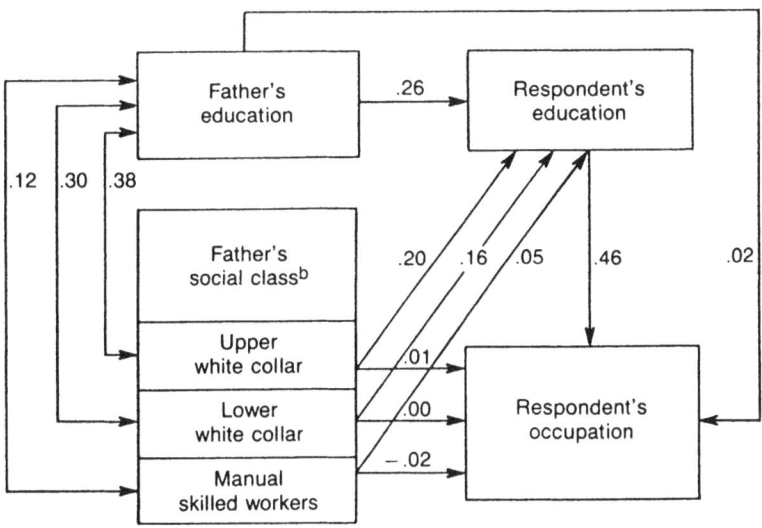

Figure 1. Standardized regression coefficients for Polish men and women, aged 30 to 39 in 1972, controlled for sex and age.[a]

[a]Pohoski et al. (1978: Tables 8.1 and 7).

[b]The class "Other manual workers" is not shown since it is used as a reference category for dummy variables describing father's social class.

trajectories of children whose class origins are intelligentsia, working class, and farmer. For ease of comparison, at the beginning of the selection process, the size of each of the three groups of children is standardized to one hundred. The table shows a decrease in the number of children with each step of educational selection. For example, of the sixteen farmers' children who graduated from high school, six took the competitive entrance examination to college, and of these only three were admitted. For children of the intelligentsia the comparable numbers are 47, 35, and 17. Thus the table can be interpreted as showing the educational advantages of children of the intelligentsia. The children of workers and farmers are somewhat compensated for these disadvantages by other educational channels (e.g., evening schools, part-time study) or by continuing education after some years of full-time employment. However, even if all roads to

Table 5

Educational Selection for the Cohort of All Elementary School Graduates in 1970, by Social Class Origin[a]

Social class origin	Graduates of elementary school	Admitted to 4 or 5 year high school	Graduated from high school	Took competitive exams to college or university	Admitted to college or university
Intelligentsia N = 2,580[b]	100	58	47	35	17
Working class N = 4,440[b]	100	30	29	12	5
Farmers N = 2,980[b]	100	21	16	6	3

[a]Based on Białecki, 1982: Tables 3, 4, 5.
[b]After standardization to 100,000 for three classes (intelligentsia, working class, and farmers) together.

educational attainment are taken into account, inequality of educational opportunity is still substantial, as evidenced by cohort analysis (Pohoski, 1984) and analysis of diachronic statistics (Jarosz, 1984).

Recently Misztal (1984) showed that an important determinant of the level of education attained is the extent to which a person believes that education is instrumental in obtaining social rewards. Using loglinear analysis she demonstrates that the instrumental view of education depends on a person's total value system. However, both variables depend on the level of the parents' education. Using sociopsychological techniques Misztal provides an explanatory model of the reproduction of educational capital at the individual rather than the institutional level.

Psychological aspects of social stratification

All the papers in this volume except that by Słomczyński contain data on the perception of social differentiation or on value preferences. Interest in the psychological aspects of social stratification, attributable to the influence of Ossowski's (1963) work, is a characteristic of Polish sociological research. This interest extends to political sociology, a highly active research area that is beyond the scope of the present volume.

Educational and occupational prestige

A recent book by Wejland (1983) is devoted to the semantic analysis of the concept of prestige. Wejland shows that the essence of prestige is the relation of the evaluator (X) to the object being evaluated (Y). The relation contains three components: cognitive (X perceives that Y has property W); evaluative (property W has a value for X); and affective (X has a permanent positive appreciation for Y). The class of objects Y is open; it includes such units of sociological analysis as social roles, formal organizations, social groups, etc. Wejland's book makes it apparent that many categories of social objects have not yet been empirically analyzed with respect to prestige.

In this volume Sawiński's paper marks a new departure in the empirical investigation of prestige: he constructs a prestige scale of types and levels of education. In this pioneering work Sawiński shows that his scale is basically unidimensional, roughly corresponding to the number of years of formal schooling. However, it can be observed that noncompletion of an educational track (e.g., not receiving a diploma from a vocational school) is a handicap, since the assigned prestige is lower than would be expected on the basis of years of schooling. This feature of the scale may be interpreted as evidence of the social acceptance of educational credentialism, which makes diplomas essential.

Sawiński relates his empirical results on educational prestige to occupational prestige. The hierarchy of educational categories is to a great extent consistent with the hierarchy of occupational prestige. It is implicit in Sawiński's argument that educational and occupational prestige are dual aspects of a common, more general dimension of stratification.

Occupational prestige has been intensively studied in Poland since the first survey conducted in Warsaw in 1958 (Sarapata and

Table 6

Prestige Scores of Major Occupational Groups in Poland, 1958–78

Major occupational groups	Warsaw sample 1958[b]	Eleven surveys 1958–73[b]	National sample 1975[c]	Occupational prestige scale, 1978[d]
Professionals[a]	82.7	82.5	77.8	80.1
Technicians	77.5	75.1	68.0	74.6
Office workers	58.2	59.0	58.9	61.1
Foremen	71.0	69.5	66.1	67.3
Service workers	52.0	52.9	52.1	55.4
Skilled workers	75.0	69.5	67.0	64.3
Unskilled workers	38.5	46.4	47.0	38.5
Farmers	64.0	64.5	58.2	62.2
Farm laborers	37.0	41.2	46.0	36.4
Entrepreneurs	49.1	49.9	51.9	48.6

[a]Including managers.
[b]Based on Wesołowski and Słomczyński, 1977: Table 3.
[c]Based on Pohoski et al., 1976: Table 11.
[d]Based on Słomczyński and Kacprowicz, 1979: Appendix. The metric of the scale is transformed to the metric of previous studies.

Wesołowski, 1961). Since then there have been several studies carried out in cities, one study in rural areas, and one on a national sample (for review see Wesołowski and Słomczyński, 1977:78–81 and Pohoski et al., 1976:63–69). The occupational hierarchies revealed in these studies are substantially similar, at least in broad outline. The average inter-study correlation of eleven occupational prestige scales is .94.

Table 6 summarizes data from the most important studies of occupational prestige in Poland. Prestige scores for occupational groups shown in this table were calculated on the basis of ratings assigned to the occupational titles contained in each group. For comparative purposes the scores are transformed to a common metric standard. The first three columns in the table show scores obtained from the surveys, while the last column gives values of the Standard Occupational Prestige Scale for Poland, based on a study conducted among labor-force experts and university students. The standard Polish Scale (Słomczyński and Kacprowicz,

1979) provides ratings for all detailed occupational categories of the Social Classification of Occupations (Pohoski and Słomczyński, 1978). The values of this scale are adjusted to reflect the ratings of the total adult population. They are in close agreement with all other Polish studies. The average correlation between values of the Polish Scale and prestige scores from previous studies is .86, indicating the high reliability of the scale.

In each column of Table 6 the ranking is almost the same: professionals, technicians, foremen, skilled workers, individual farm owners, office workers, service workers, craftsmen, unskilled workers, farm laborers. This ordering is somewhat different from the ranking of the same occupational groups in Western Europe and the United States: skilled workers have a decisively higher ranking in Poland, while office workers have a somewhat lower ranking. Sarapata and Wesołowski (1961) have attempted to explain the relatively high ranking given to skilled workers by pointing to the influence of the socialist value system and the ideological importance attributed to productive manual work in the nationalized economy.

A study by Jakubowicz (1968) shows that the average correlation of the occupational prestige hierarchy in Poland with those in capitalist countries is .76, significantly lower than that for the capitalist countries alone (.87). The correlation of Treiman's International Prestige Scale with the scale developed for Poland is lower than with scales developed for various capitalist countries (Treiman, 1977, p. 176). Treiman's Scale measures a more universal pattern of occupational prestige than does the Polish Scale, which reflects changes within Polish society after the Second World War. It has been shown, however, that both Treiman's Scale and the Polish Scale are valid measures of the occupational status of men in Poland (Słomczyński et al., 1981:728).

Reszke (1984) takes a thoroughly up-to-date approach to occupational prestige, concentrating on questions that are important not only for sociologists but for feminists as well. The results of her survey show that men and women in Poland view some occupations as masculine and others as feminine. The social perception of an occupation as feminine diminishes its prestige. The status of a working wife is more often evaluated on the basis of her own traits than on those of her husband; at the same time, however, the status of a working wife is evaluated on the basis of the husband's traits more often than the status of a working husband is evaluated on the basis of the wife's traits.

Class images

In this volume Janicka details changes in the popular perception of the bases of social differentiation in 1965, 1976, and 1980. The change between 1976 and 1980 was greater than that between 1965 and 1976; the change in the latter period had the potential to generate social conflict, since the dimension of power came to be perceived as highly divisive. At the end of 1980 social disparities in income and the distribution of power were perceived as engendering conflict by at least 80 percent of the respondents.

Janicka's findings are consistent with the results of a secondary analysis by Koralewicz-Zębik, summarized in her survey paper, "The perception of inequality in Poland 1965–1980." She clearly demostrates that "over time the vertical division of society came to prevail, becoming clearly dominant in the late 1970s."

> It seems that in the 1970s the perception among Poles of structural inequality was becoming more common as well as more dichotomous. In the studies by the Center for Research on Public Opinion in 1980, answers to an open question about the most striking differences and inequalities in Poland revealed a perception of the social structure in which there are inequalities between those who have high incomes and the rest of the society, between those who have good connections in high places and the rest of the society, and between the privileged professional groups (the police and the army) and the rest of the society. (p. 230)

That such a dichotomous image of class structure prevailed in the late 1970s and early 1980s is shown by other studies as well

Table 7

Percentage of Respondents Who Say That a Given Social Difference Strongly Divides People in Society

In your opinion, which of these differences divide people in our society?	National sample 1962[a]	Warsaw sample, 1973[b]		National sample 1975[c]
		Parents	Children	
Differences in income or wealth	82	81	72	92
Differences in education	71	48	42	76
Differences between supervisory and subordinate positions	64	63	60	79
Differences between nonmanual and manual work	57	42	45	66
Differences in manner of behaving in company	57	62	71	48
Differences in religious outlook	48	32	32	32
Differences in political views	47	54	60	24
Differences resulting from living in urban versus rural areas	44	46	68	59
Differences in class origin	23	27	34	28
Differences between party members and others	—	32	38	—

[a]Nowak, 1969: Table 7.
[b]Nowak, 1976: Table 12.
[c]Nowak, 1981: p. 50.

(Beskid, 1982; Kolarska and Rychard, 1982).

In this volume Zaborowski analyzes the determinants and consequences of dichotomous class images. In the light of previous studies, such a focus of his work is well justified. Zaborowski's contribution consists in showing that in socialist Poland the perception of class structure as dichotomous is an integral part of workers' radicalism.

Among many studies devoted to perception of the bases of

social differentiation, only a few allow for direct diachronic comparison. The three surveys of Nowak (1969, 1976, 1981) contain questions of the following kind: "In your opinion, which social differences divide people in our society?" In Table 7 we present the results of these surveys for nine characteristics.

Nowak (1981:50) summarizes the results as follows:

> In 1961 differences in earnings or wealth were cited by more than 80 percent of the respondents as a divisive influence; by 1975 the proportion had increased to more than 90 percent. Other factors that bear directly on social standing, such as education and kind of work, were also selected more frequently in the later survey. Meanwhile, differences in personal behavior, in religious outlook, and in political views diminished in importance.

We should also point out that in the 1973 Warsaw sample a relatively small proportion of respondents mentioned differences between party members and others as the basis for important social divisions.

Various surveys in Poland show a significant correlation between socioeconomic status and class self-identification (for a review see Wesołowski and Słomczyński, 1977:86–8). In this volume Słomczyński and Kacprowicz analyze the relationship between objective social status and its subjective evaluation. A large part of their paper is devoted to constructing synthetic measures of respondents' assessments of their positions in such categories as education, occupational skills, manual/nonmanual nature of work, role in the decision-making process, prestige, income, and participation in cultural life. At the beginning of the 1980s the variables defining objective social status explained about 60 percent of the variance of globally measured subjective status.

In their papers both Janicka and Zaborowski consider egalitarian attitudes toward the distribution of income. Much research in Poland has been devoted to this topic (Nowak, 1960; Malewski, 1971; Wesołowski and Krauze, 1980; Wesołowski, 1980; Blachnicki, 1978, 1979); it shows that people opt for a narrow range of income inequality. From the data presented by Janicka and Zaborowski it appears that Poles favor a redistribution of income simply for the sake of egalitarianism. For example, the response to the statement "The highest earnings should be reduced even if this would not lead to an increase in the lowest earnings" is largely affirmative. However, at the same time Poles favor meritocratic allocation of earnings, that is, an allocation based on knowledge, occupational skills, and formal education (Blachnicki, 1979; Wesołowski and Krauze, 1980). These results point out an inconsistency in public opinion for which a theoretically satisfactory explanation has not yet been provided (cf. Phillips, 1983).

In this volume Krauze and Słomczyński investigate another subjective aspect of social inequality. Two problems are empirically approached: people's perception of social mobility and their evaluation of it in terms of their sense of social justice. The results should be seen as suggestive rather than conclusive, since they are based on a small sample of university students. Unexpectedly, students sense more injustice than acually exists according to their own equity standards.

Stratification and the system of values

Empirical research typically shows that the system of values is not strongly differentiated with respect to occupational groups or social classes. In Poland, values connected with individualism (the private sphere of life, including family and friends) are highly prominent, as are democratic values (including egalitarianism and concern and respect for human dignity). Since these values are shared across age strata, it has been argued that they account for the low intensity of intergenerational conflict (Nowak, 1979; 1981; see also Koralewicz-Zębik, 1979).

In this volume Misztal analyzes four values: happy family life, educational achievement, high income, and altruistic social action. She shows that preferences among these four values are rather modestly differentiated with respect to occupational groupings. Educational achievement and altruistic social action appear to be most frequently preferred by nonmanual workers; manual workers tend to value income more highly and, in turn, give lower ranking to educational achievement and altruistic social action.

Wiśniewski (1981) considered the place of power, welfare, and education in the Polish system of values. Among these values, power has a considerably lower ranking than the other two; this is true for all occupational groups. Managers value power more than any other group does. It is also apparent that the less education required for a respondent's occupation, the higher the probability that he or she considers material goods worth obtaining.

Other recent studies on the relationship between the system of values and the social structure use qualitative approaches (Marody and Nowak, 1983; Narojek, 1982; Szawiel, 1982). They reveal how systems of values are connected with the specific interests of competing social groups, and describe confrontational social situations that crystallize previously amorphous values. For example, during the strikes of 1980, managers defended values that were functional for their retention of privileged positions, while workers upheld values that promoted human dignity (Marody and Nowak, 1983:16). Such tense situations, where group action for the defense of certain values is exhibited, provide research opportunities for insight into the coherence of the value system as a whole.

In 1972-73 Nowak (1976) conducted a study of the system of values among high school students and their parents in two cities. Two conclusions emerged: first, values were weakly correlated with variables describing social stratification; second, there was a weak correlation between the values of parents and those of their children. Both conclusions were subsequently questioned with respect to the values related to self-direction, as conceptualized by Kohn (1969; Kohn and Schooler, 1983). Koralewicz-Zębik (1982) analyzed parental values and showed that valuing self-direction for children depends significantly on a person's education, occupation, and income. (For a similar analysis see Słomczyński *et al.*, 1981). Kohn *et al.* (1986) demonstrated that in Poland the correlation between the valuation of self-direction by parents and their children is much higher than could be expected on the basis of the Polish, Western European, and American literature.

* * *

Using the papers included in this volume as a point of departure, we have briefly surveyed some of the contributions made by Polish sociologists in the field of social stratification. The record indicates that the field is well established and productive. Moreover, the results of Polish research can be used for comparison with other stratification patterns. Further development of the field is to be anticipated.

This volume does not pretend to represent the entire spectrum of current Polish research on social stratification. Several complementary sources are available in English. The reader may consult *The Polish Sociological Bulletin*, a quarterly published since 1961, and a new journal, *Sisyphus*, whose entire third volume, published in 1982, is devoted to the crises and conflicts in Poland during 1980-81. Polish sociologists have presented more than twenty papers at meetings of the Research Committee on Social Stratification of the International Sociological Association over the last five years. A number of relevant journal articles by Polish sociologists, cited above, are available in English, as are several theoretical works. Among the latter, those by Wesołowski (1979), Staniszkis (1983), and Nowak (1983) are examples of divergent interests. Four volumes devoted to empirical cross-country comparative research are available: Rutkevich and Wesołowski (1974), Allardt and Wesołowski (1978), Wnuk-Lipiński and Kolosi (1984), and Andorka and Zagórski (1980). Finally, we note some informative books specifically devoted to the empirical study of social stratification in Poland, written by sociologists who work outside Poland: Lane and Kolankiewicz (1973), Tellenback (1975), and Matejko (1974).

Bibliography

Alestalo, M., K. M. Słomczyński and W. Wesołowski
1978   "Patterns of social stratification." Pp. 117–46 in E. Allardt and W. Wesołowski (eds.), *Social Structure and Change. Finland and Poland in Comparative Perspective*. Warsaw: Polish Scientific Publishers.

Allardt, E. and W. Wesołowski (eds.)
1978   *Social Structure and Change. Finland and Poland in Comparative Perspective*. Warsaw: Polish Scientific Publishers.

Andorka, R. and K. Zagórski
1980   *Socio-occupational Mobility in Hungary and Poland*. Warsaw: Institute of Philosophy and Sociology of the Polish Academy of Sciences.

Beskid, L.
1982   "Pay and income as factors in the crisis." *Sisyphus* 3:149–59.

Białecki, I.
1982   *Wybór szkoły a reprodukcja struktury społecznej*. [School Selection and Reproduction of Social Structure.] Wrocław: Ossolineum.

Blachnicki, B.
1978   "Economic equality in the consciousness of industrial employees." Pp. 193–205 in Polish Sociological Association (ed.), *Social Structure*. Wrocław: Ossolineum.
1979   *Pracownicy przemysłu wobec egalitaryzmu*. [Industrial Employees and Egalitarianism.] Wrocław: Ossolineum.

Connor, W. D.
1979   *Socialism, Politics, and Equality*. New York: Columbia University Press.

Domański, H.
1983   "Klasyfikacja zawodów jako narzędzie analizy systemu uwarstwienia społecznego." [Classification of occupations as a tool of analysis of the system of social stratification.] *Studia Socjologiczne* No. 2(89):251–69.

Domański, H. and Z. Sawiński
1984   "Prestiż i pozycja społeczna jako wymiary ruchliwości zawodowej." [Prestige and social position as dimensions of occupational mobility.] *Studia Socjologiczne* No.2(93):107–25.

Drążkiewicz, J.
1980   "Development of social structure and the concept of interest." *Polish Sociological Bulletin* No. 1(149):23–38.

Erikson, R., J. H. Goldthorpe, and L. Portocarero
1982   "Social fluidity in industrial nations." *British Journal of Sociology* 33:1–34.

Featherman, D. L., F. L. Jones, and R. M. Hauser
    1975   "Assumptions of social mobility research in the U.S.: the case of occupational status." *Social Science Research* 4:329-60.

Goodman, L.
    1969   "How to ransack social mobility tables and other kinds of cross-classification tables." *American Journal of Sociology* 75:1-40.

Goyder, J.
    1984   "Social mobility or status attainment or social mobility and status attainment?" *Canadian Review of Sociology and Anthropology* 21(No.3):331-43.

Hauser, R. M.
    1978   "A structural model of the mobility table." *Social Forces* 56:919-50.

Hochfeld, J.
    1956   "On the programme of research on the formation of new worker milieus in People's Poland." Pp. 121-9 in *Transactions of the Third World Congress of Sociology*, Vol. 7. London.
    1963   *Studia o marksowskiej teorii społeczeństwa.* [Studies on Marxian Theory of Society.] Warsaw: Polish Scientific Publishers.
    1967   "The concept of class interest." *Polish Sociological Bulletin*, No. 2:5-14.

Hryniewicz, T.
    1983   "Metodologiczne aspekty analizy struktury klasowej w Polsce. Stosunki produkcji, władza, klasy społeczne." [Methodological aspects of the analysis of class structure in Poland. Relations of production; power; social classes.] *Studia Socjologiczne* No. 1(88):43-73.

Jakubowicz, M.
    1968   "Comparative studies of occupational hierarchies." *Co-existence* 5:63-83.

Jarosz, M.
    1984   *Nierówności społeczne.* [Social inequalities.] Warsaw: Książka i Wiedza.

Jasińska, A. and L. Nowak
    1973   "Foundations of Marx's theory of class: a reconstruction." Pp. 141-69 in P. K. Crosser (ed.), *East-West Dialogues*. Amsterdam.

Klatzky, S. and R. M. Hodge
    1971   "A canonical correlation analysis of occupational mobility." *Journal of the American Statistical Association* 66:16-22.

Kohn, M. L.
    1969   *Class and Conformity: A Study in Values*. Homewood, Ill.: The Dorsey Press.

Kohn, M. L. and C. Schooler (with the collaboration of J. Miller, K. A. Miller, C. Schoenbach and R. Schoenberg)
    1984   *Work and Personality: An Inquiry into the Impact of Social Stratification*. Norwood, N.J.: Ablex.

Kohn, M., K. M. Słomczyński, and C. Schoenbach

1986 "Social stratification and the transmission of values in the family: a cross-national assessment." *Sociological Forum* I, No. 1.

Kolarska, L. and A. Rychard
1982 "Visions of social order." *Sisyphus* 3:206-23.

Koralewicz-Zębik, J.
1979 "Niektóre przemiany systemu wartości, celów i orientacji życiowych społeczeństwa polskiego." [Some changes in value systems, life orientations, and individual goals in Polish society.] *Studia Socjologiczne* No. 4(75):175-90.
1982 "Wartości rodzicielskie a stratyfikacja społeczna." [Parental values and social stratification.]. *Studia Socjologiczne* No. 3-4(86-7):237-62.
1984 "The perception of inequality in Poland, 1956-1980." *Sociology* 18(May):225-38.

Kozyr-Kowalski, S.
1970 "Marx's theory of classes and social strata and 'Capital'." *Polish Sociological Bulletin*, No. 1:17-32.

Krauze, T. and K. M. Słomczyński
1986 "Matrix representation of structural and circulation mobility." *Sociological Methods and Research* 14, No. 3.

Ładosz, J.
1977 "Contradictions in the development of socialist society." *Dialectics and Humanism* 4:83-93.

Lane, D. and G. Kolankiewicz (eds.)
1973 *Social Groups in Polish Society*. New York: Columbia University Press.

Malewski, A.
1971 "Attitudes of the employees from Warsaw enterprises toward differentiation of wages and the social system in May 1958." *The Polish Sociological Bulletin*, No. 2:5-21.

Marody M. and K. Nowak
1983 "Wartości i działania. O niektórych teoretycznych i metodologicznych problemach badania wartości i ich związków z działaniem." [Values and actions. On some theoretical and methodological problems in the investigation of values and their relationship to actions.] *Studia Socjologiczne* No. 4(91):5-30.

Matejko, A.
1974 *Social Change and Stratification in Eastern Europe: An Interpretative Analysis of Poland and Her Neighbors*. New York: Praeger.

Misztal, M.
1984 "Społeczno-psychologiczne aspekty reprodukcji struktury edukacyjnej w Polsce." [Socio-psychological aspects of the reproduction of the educational structure in Poland.] *Studia Socjologiczne* No. 2(93):87-106.

Narojek, W.
1982 *Struktura społeczna w doświadczeniu jednostki*. [Social Structure in the Individual's Experience.] Warsaw: State Publishing House.

Nowak, L.
1983 *Property and Power. Towards a Non-Marxian Historical Materialism.* Boston: Reidel.
Nowak, S.
1960 "Egalitarian attitudes of Warsaw students." *American Sociological Review* 25:219-31.
1969 "Changes in social structure in social consciousness." Pp. 235-47 in C. S. Heller (ed.), *Structural Social Inequality.* New York: Macmillan.
1979 "System wartości społeczeństwa polskiego." [The value system of Polish society.] *Studia Socjologiczne* No. 4(75):155-73.
1981 "Values and attitudes of the Polish people." *Scientific American* 245(No. 1):45-53.
Nowak, S. (ed.)
1976 *Ciągłość i zmiana tradycji kulturowej.* [Continuity and Change of Cultural Tradition.] Warsaw: University of Warsaw Press.
Ossowski, S.
1963 *Class Structure in the Social Consciousness.* London: Routledge and Kegan Paul (1957).
Phillips, D.
1983 "The normative standing of economic inequalities." *Sociologische Gids* 30 (September):318-50.
Pohoski, M.
1984 "Kariery szkolne i kariery społeczno-zawodowe a pochodzenie społeczne." [School careers and socio-occupational careers versus social origins.] *Kultura i Społeczeństwo,* No. 2(28):155-72.
Pohoski, M., K. M. Słomczyński, and K. Milczarek
1974 *Społeczna klasyfikacja zawodów.* [Social Classification of Occupations.] Warsaw: Institute of Philosophy and Sociology of the Polish Academy of Sciences.
Pohoski, M., K. M. Słomczyński, and W. Wesołowski
1976 "Occupational prestige in Poland 1958-1975." *Polish Sociological Bulletin,* No. 4:63-77.
Pohoski, M. and K. M. Słomczyński
1978 *Społeczna klasyfikacja zawodów.* [Social Classification of Occupations.] Warsaw: Institute of Philosophy and Sociology of the Polish Academy of Sciences.
Pohoski, M., S. Pontinen, and K. Zagórski
1978 "Social mobility and socio-economic achievement." Pp. 147-82 in E. Allardt and W. Wesołowski (eds.), *Social Structure and Change. Finland and Poland in Comparative Perspective.* Warsaw: Polish Scientific Publishers.
Polish Sociological Assocation (ed.)
1978 *Social Structure. Polish Sociology 1977.* Wrocław: Ossolineum.
Reszke, I.
1984 *Prestiż społeczny a płeć. Kryteria prestiżu zawodów i osób.* [Social Prestige and Gender. Criteria of Prestige of Occupations and Per-

sons.] Wrocław: Ossolineum.
Rutkevich, M. N. and W. Wesołowski (eds.)
    1974   *Transformations of Social Structure in the USSR and Poland.* Moscow and Warsaw: USSR and Polish Academies of Sciences.
Sarapata, A. and W. Wesołowski
    1961   "The evaluation of occupations by Warsaw inhabitants." *American Journal of Sociology* 66:581-91.
Słomczyński, K. M., and T. Krauze (eds.)
    1978   *Class Structure and Social Mobility in Poland.* White Plains, N.Y.: M. E. Sharpe.
Słomczyński, K. M. and G. Kacprowicz
    1979   *Skale zawodów.* [Scales of Occupations.] Warsaw: Institute of Philosophy and Sociology of the Polish Academy of Sciences.
Słomczyński, K. M., J. Miller, and M. L. Kohn
    1981   "Stratification, work, and values: a Polish-United States comparison." *American Sociological Review* 46:720-44.
Staniszkis, J.
    1983   *Poland's Self-Limiting Revolution.* Princeton: Princeton University Press.
Szawiel, T.
    1982   "Struktura społeczna i postawy a grupy ethosowe." [Social structure and attitudes versus ethos groups.] *Studia Socjologiczne* No. 1-2.
Szczepański, J.
    1970   *Polish Society.* New York: Random House.
    1978   "Early stages of socialist industrialization and changes in social class structure." Pp. 11-36 in K. M. Słomczyński and T. Krauze (eds.), *Class Structure and Social Stratification in Poland.* White Plains: M. E. Sharpe.
Tellenback, S.
    1975   *The Social Structure of Socialist Society. The Polish Interpretation.* Lund: Studentlitteratur.
Treiman, D. J.
    1977   *Occupational Prestige in Comparative Perspective.* New York: Academic Press.
Wejland, A. P.
    1983   *Prestiż: analiza struktur pojęciowych.* [Prestige: An Analysis of Conceptual Structures.] Warsaw: Institute of Philosophy and Sociology of the Polish Academy of Sciences.
Wesołowski, W.
    1967   "Marx's theory of class domination. An attempt at systematization." *Polish Round Table* 1:21-53.
    1969   "Strata and strata interests in socialist society. Toward a new theoretical approach." Pp. 465-77 in C. S. Heller (ed.), *Structured Social Inequality.* New York: Macmillan.
    1979   *Class, Strata, and Power.* London: Routledge and Kegan Paul.
    1980   "Stratification and meritocratic justice." In D. J. Treiman (ed.),

Research on Social Stratification and Mobility. Greenwich, Conn.: JAI Press.

Wesołowski, W. (ed.)
1970 Zróżnicowanie społeczne. [Social Differentiation.] Wrocław: Ossolineum.

Wesołowski, W. and T. K. Krauze
1980 "Socialist society and the meritocratic principle of remuneration." Pp. 337–48 in G. Berreman (ed.), Social Inequality: Comparative and Developmental Approaches. New York: Academic Press.

Wesołowski, W. and K. M. Słomczyński
1977 Investigations on Class Structure and Social Stratification in Poland: 1945–1975. Warsaw: Institute of Philosophy and Sociology of the Polish Academy of Sciences.

Widerszpil, S.
1978 "Problems in the theory of the development of a socialist society." Polish Sociological Bulletin, No. 2:23–36.

Wiśniewski, W.
1981 "Power, welfare, and education in the Polish value system." Polish Sociological Bulletin, No. 1(53):37–46.

Wnuk-Lipiński, E. and T. Kolosi (eds.)
1984 Equality and Inequality under Socialism. Poland and Hungary Compared. Beverly Hills, Ca.: Sage.

Zagórski, K.
1971 "Podział ludności na grupy społeczno-zawodowe w NSP 1970." [Division of the population into socio-economic groups in the national census of 1970.] Wiadomości Statystyczne No. 5:6–7.

1976 Zmiany struktury i ruchliwość społeczno-zawodowa w Polsce. [Changes of Structure and Socio-occupational Mobility in Poland.] Warsaw: Central Statistical Office.

Social Inequality and Social Mobility

MICHAŁ POHOSKI

Theoretical background

In this article we examine social inequality of "life chances," that is, in Giddens's words, "the chances an individual has of sharing in the socially created economic and cultural goods which typically exist in any given society" (Giddens, 1973: 130). Inequality of life chances can be approached from two perspectives, corresponding to different aspects of the stratification system: (1) the division of goods between social groups or categories and (2) the access of individuals to the same groups. Specific theories of stratification, as well as ideologies addressing the issue of social inequality, usually emphasize one of these two aspects.

The Marxist approach is concerned above all with the creation and transformation of class inequality resulting from the division of goods.[1] By contrast, the functional approach emphasizes individuals' inequality of access to hierarchically ordered social posi-

---

This research was carried out by the Social Mobility Research Group of the Institute of Sociology, University of Warsaw, under my direction, with the assistance of the Institute of Philosophy and Sociology of the Polish Academy of Sciences. The subject of research was the "life history" of persons who began their occupational careers and, in the majority of cases, their schooling, after World War II (the oldest were born in 1933 and the youngest in 1942). A comprehensive characterization of the sample, its method of selection, and its representativeness can be found in Lissowski (1976). In 1976 the same type of research was conducted among Warsaw residents. A comparison of the results of both surveys indicates great similarities in social mobility (Jaźwińska-Motylska, 1982).

tions. Both aspects are included in the theoretical conceptualization recently developed by Parkin (1974: 1-18).[2] Following this conceptualization, Weber's concept of "social closure" is used, indicating the process by which social collectivities strive to maximize their benefits by restricting direct access to rewards and limiting the opportunities for obtaining them.

Parkin analyzes two strategies utilized in social closure. The first is exclusion, applied by the privileged groups; it involves the adoption of specific means to control access to rewards and opportunities. Opposed to it is the strategy of usurpation, utilized by disadvantaged groups against privileged ones; it entails a questioning of existing norms for the distribution of goods. The effectiveness of usurpation depends on the ability of disadvantaged groups to achieve social mobilization of their members.

While exclusion has, as a rule, the support of the state and does not require personal sacrifice on the part of the members of privileged groups, the actions of disadvantaged groups do not receive such support and do demand personal sacrifice. Techniques of exclusion have a stabilizing (conservative) impact on the system of inequalities; those of usurpation, which bring into question existing norms of distribution, lead to changes in the system.

This theoretical conceptualization subsumes, on the one hand, the distribution of goods among social groups and, on the other, the distribution of individuals among these groups. Most important in this approach is linking these processes in order to indicate their dependence. Consistent with the postulated dependence, the factors that govern the distribution of social goods between groups will also determine individuals' affiliations to these groups. In other words, the power of social groups is reflected in both the distribution of goods and the distribution of individuals among groups—that is, in the process of class formation.

In line with this, empirical research on social stratification ought not only to examine the nature of the distribution of goods and the nature of the processes of sorting individuals among social groups, but should also identify the reciprocal relations between these processes. For Parkin, the strategy of exclusion, adopted by privileged groups, and the strategy of usurpation, adopted by disadvantaged groups, reflect class conflict, which constitutes the main force of social change. As Goldthorpe (1980:38) makes clear, analysis of the amount and patterns of social mobility should allow us to evaluate (1) the effectiveness of exclusion and (2) the likelihood of success of the contrary strategy. The effectiveness of the latter "must depend on participants being ready to opt for collective interests and aspirations rather than individual ones."

Data on socio-occupational categories

Poland's stratification system is shaped by two principal mechanisms: central planning and the market—in particular, the labor market.[3] The dominant role of central planning in determining socioeconomic objectives, assigning economic functions, and providing resources increases the significance of political, economic, and administrative power in shaping the system of social inequalities. The ability to influence the plan constitutes an ability to affect the system of social relations and inequalities (Narojek, 1973). In turn, the position of individuals and groups in the labor market depends on the ownership of the means of production, as well as on skills, occupational qualifications, and other factors.

In this paper, I distinguish social groups[4] by examining the division of labor that is reflected in the occupational structure (Blau and Duncan, 1967; Parkin, 1971; Wesołowski, 1975). In particular, I make use of the Social Classification of Occupations (Pohoski and Słomczyński, 1978). This classification distinguished over two hundred narrowly specific occupational categories, aggregated according to the following criteria: the nature of the activity performed, manual (blue-collar) versus nonmanual (white-collar) type of work, level of occupational skills required, function performed, enterprise in which the work is performed (state-run or not), and relation to the means of production (hired labor, independent, or employed in a small family enterprise).

Using these criteria we arrived at twelve broad occupational categories:

1) professionals, i.e. technical and nontechnical specialists (e.g., doctors, lawyers, writers, teachers, biologists);
2) managers, including high-level officials in state administration, political and social organizations;
3) semiprofessionals, i.e., technicians and specialized white-collar workers (e.g., nurses, accountants, inspectors);
4) office workers (e.g., clerks, cashiers, typists);
5) service workers (employees combining nonmanual and manual work, e.g., shop assistants, waiters, conductors);
6) owners of manufacturing, trade, and service enterprises (e.g., shop owners, self-employed artisans);
7) foremen (blue-collar workers who are first-line supervisors);
8) skilled manual workers (e.g., miners, steelworkers, lathe operators, locksmiths);
9) semiskilled manual workers (i.e., workers performing preparatory and complementary tasks);
10) unskilled manual workers (i.e., workers without any specialization who perform only simple tasks);
11) farmers and family members who assist them;
12) agricultural laborers (employed by state farms and by private farmers).

The data for our analysis of social inequality and social mobility are taken from a "life history" research project. A national random sample of 9,000 men and 4,000 women was used. The respondents were between 30 and 39 years of age and had been occupationally active for at least two months in 1972. Excluded from the sample were military and security personnel.

In addition to the national survey I consider another sample, involving a group that is important in the processes of social stratification and mobility yet relatively underrepresented in the national study—directors and high ranking administrative man-

Table 1

Selected Socioeconomic Characteristics of Occupational Groups. Polish Men and Women Aged 30 to 39 in 1972

Occupational groups	Years of school-ing	Books[a]	Earnings from main job[b]	Per capita family income[b]	Percent of families below social minimum	Percent of families having good housing condi-tions	Percent of families owning a car	Percent of party (PUWP) members	Percent of party (PUWP) activists[c]	Average prestige score[d]	High self-evalua-tion of social status[e]	Lack of influence in work-place[f]
(0) Directors[g]	15.0	—[h]	7.6	3.5	—	74	58	90	60	—	72	—
(1) Profes-sionals	12.3	4	4.3	2.1	6	71	28	48	14	57	37	40
(2) Managers	12.4	5	4.8	2.2	8	76	32	69	26	64	51	13
(3) Semipro-fessionals	10.9	7	3.6	1.9	8	67	15	40	14	39	22	46
(4) Office workers	10.1	13	2.9	1.6	23	45	13	38	11	39	28	47
(5) Service workers	8.1	33	2.6	1.3	38	26	6	26	3	27	11	54

(6) Owners	8.4	17	4.1	1.6	26	47	50	8	1	29	15	10
(7) Foremen	8.3	26	3.8	1.6	17	48	8	30	7	40	15	53
(8) Skilled manual workers	7.9	35	3.4	1.4	27	37	7	18	3	27	13	63
(9) Semi-skilled manual workers	6.9	53	2.6	1.2	43	18	2	15	3	19	10	71
(10) Unskilled manual workers	6.8	57	2.6	1.2	45	16	1	12	1	16	8	77
(11) Farmers	6.4	54	—	—	—	6	6	11	2	19	16	12
(12) Agricultural laborers	6.6	55	2.8	.9	58	9	3	33	5	19	14	62

[a] — Percent of families having no books at home (other than school texts).
[b] — In thousands of zlotys per month.
[c] — Activists are defined as those who hold an unpaid party post.
[d] — Mean score on the scale of socioeconomic status.
[e] — Percent of those who evaluate their own status as being above average.
[f] — Percent of people who answered they had little or not influence on matters affecting their workplace.
[g] — Only directors employed in Warsaw.
[h] — No reliable data.

agers. Given the difficulty of obtaining a national random sample of this group, the study is limited to a sample of 261 directors and managers based in Warsaw. It includes directors working in central administration and economic enterprises that employed at least 500 persons. The findings about this group are used (Wasilewski, 1981) to characterize its social position, located high in the hierarchy of power.

Aspects of social inequality

To what extent do members of these occupational categories differ in their "life chances?" In order to answer this question the following aspects of life chances are considered: (a) access to knowledge and information; (b) standard of living; (c) power; (d) prestige and other subjective dimensions of social position. Data on these aspects of life chances are presented in Table 1. In this table the group of "high-ranking" directors is added to the twelve occupational groups.

The indices presented in Table 1 are by no means uniform. Owning a car is a more specific aspect of social position than housing conditions or a living standard below the social minimum. These last two indicators have a particular social significance since they involve the satisfaction of people's basic needs (Maslow, 1943). Therefore they are constructed as synthetic indices.

Inequality in access to knowledge and information

An individual's educational level can be regarded as the most important indicator of his or her access to knowledge and information (Kłoskowska, 1981: 449, 481-7). As can be seen from data characterizing average educational level (measured by the number of years of schooling), the gap between the "extreme" categories is substantial. In general, directors have had at least some university education, while the average educational level of agricultural laborers is nearly half a grade less than the number of grades in primary school (seven grades).

Obviously the use of average levels blurs differences between groups. Full data on educational levels indicate that distributions of this variable overlap to a great degree, especially among "neighboring" groups. But even here differences are quite marked, especially (a) between white- and blue-collar workers and (b) between skilled and unskilled workers in nonagricultural and agricultural sectors.

There are also major differences in the number of books owned by the various groups. A majority of the private farmers and agricultural laborers, nearly half of the unskilled workers, and over 30 percent of the skilled workers do not have even one book (including textbooks) at home; among white-collar workers the proportion that do not own books fluctuates between 1 and 8 percent.

Inequality in standard of living

Among occupational groups, earnings from a person's main job[5] are less differentiated than per capita income for families.[6] The proportion of families living below the social minimum[7] ranges from several percent for the professionals and managers to nearly 60 percent for agricultural laborers. Almost half of the families of unskilled and semiskilled workers in nonagricultural sectors live below the social minumum. The figure for skilled workers is 27 percent.

Given the severity of housing problems in Poland, indices concerning them should be treated as particularly revealing. A synthetic index depicting "good" conditions in this sphere was constructed. Good conditions are those in which a family has a separate apartment that is equipped with running water and sanitation, and the number of persons per room does not exceed one. Seventy-five percent of the families of managers live in such conditions while, in contrast, only 6 percent to 9 percent of farmers or farm laborers do.

A similar pattern emerges when we look at indices for access to those goods that are regarded as luxury or quasi-luxury items in Poland—for instance, cars. However, relatively small differences appear among groups in terms of owning goods of everyday utility, such as refrigerators, radios, and televison sets. Data concerning these commodities will not be analyzed in this article.

Inequality of access to power

Although carrying out managerial functions constitutes one of the criteria used to classify occupations, I have also taken into account a series of additional indices of access to power, in particular, indices directly subsumed under job conditions. Such indices include membership in the Polish United Workers' Party (PUWP) and holding a nonpermanent post in it.[8]

Membership in the party can be treated as an index of potential access to authority[9]: it represents, after all, a necessary if not sufficient condition for acceding to various administrative managerial functions in political organizations and institutions, and in state and economic administration. Thus almost 90 percent of the group of "high-ranking" directors are members of the PUWP and an additional 3 percent are members of the United People's Party (UPP) or the Democratic Party (DP). Only 7 percent of directors do not belong to any party, while in the entire sample this proportion is about 75 percent.

Intergroup differences in membership in the PUWP are evident not only in the case of directors and managers. These differences are very marked between white- and blue-collar workers. The proportion of subordinate office personnel belonging to the party is 38 percent, while the proportion among skilled workers is much lower (18%) and among unskilled laborers lower still (12%). Among manual workers only foremen and agricultural laborers belong to the party in relatively large proportion (30–34%).

Greater differences among social groups occur in indices of real sharing in power, especially holding posts in the PUWP. The probability of a director holding such a post is 20 times greater than for a skilled worker, and over 60 times greater than for an unskilled worker. If only party members are considered, the probability of a director holding such a position is, respectively, four and seven times greater than that of someone from the other two groups.

Subjective aspects of social inequality

Table 1 includes three subjective aspects of social inequality: an approximate measure of the prestige of an occupation (Słomczyński and Kacprowicz, 1979), the respondents' perception of his or her own social status, and perceived influence in the work place. The measure of prestige represents the average scores of all occupations comprising a given category. In turn, indices of a respondent's evaluation of his or her social status and influence were based on answers to two interview questions: "What position do you think you hold in society?" and "What influence do you have on issues in your work place?"

Both the distribution of occupational prestige and respondents' subjective evaluations are consistent with objective attributes. Nearly three-quarters of the directors and over half of the managers identified their social position as above average, while the corresponding percent for other nonmanual employees ranged between 22 and 37 percent and for manual workers between 8 percent (for unskilled workers) and 16 percent (for farmers). In turn, the proportion of respondents assessing their influence on workplace issues as low varied from 13% among managers and 40–47% among the remaining nonmanual employees to 53–77% among blue-collar workers. A decisive majority of manual workers (63% of the skilled and 77% of the unskilled workers) consider their influence in the workplace to be either insignificant or nonexistent.

The hierarchy of occupational groups

Analysis of the data leads to the conclusion that occupational groups differ markedly in access to socially desired material and cultural goods, thereby constituting a relatively uniform structure of inequality. If we look at this structure in terms of continuities and discontinuities in the distribution of attributes (Ossowski, 1968), we notice that a unique place is reserved for "high-ranking" directors. They differ from people in other groups not only in terms of their position in the administrative and economic hierarchy, which was the basis for classifying them as a separate group, but also in terms of access to political power, standard of living, and, to a somewhat lesser degree, access to knowledge and information. Directors are at the top of the pyramid in all these dimensions, and they are located comparatively far from the next two groups, managers and professionals.

The next clear discontinuity in the distribution of attributes appears between blue-collar and white-collar workers. Among the former only foremen have some indices of standard of living that are higher than those for subordinate office personnel. In earnings, too, skilled workers rank higher on average than subordinate office personnel. Skilled workers rank markedly lower, however, on all other indices.

Two less evident discontinuities can also be indentified. The first is between skilled and semiskilled or unskilled manual workers employed outside of agriculture, the second between semiskilled or unskilled workers outside of agriculture and farmers or agricultural laborers. Apart from indices related to power, farmers and agricultural laborers always rank lowest.

The analysis of indices characterizing access to various socially desired goods demonstrates that the broad occupational categories distinguished here form a clearly indentifiable hierarchy. At the top we find the "power elite," represented here by directors of administrative and economic institutions, and at the bottom, unskilled laborers and farmers. It should be emphasized that this is a hierarchy of broad, not narrow, occupational categories. As

Parkin (1974: 23) correctly notes, the existence of a hierarchy of broad occupational groups does not preclude the possibility of deviations in the position of narrowly defined occupations.

Amount and directions of social mobility

The amount and directions of social mobility will be described for twelve occupational categories. The category of "high-ranking" directors, indentified by the symbol "O" in Table 1, is excluded from analysis since it is limited to the Warsaw sample. A separate work examines the social mobility of this occupational group (Wasilewski, 1981). The small number of directors in the national sample has been included in the category of "managers."

Data showing the intergenerational mobility of men are presented in Tables 2 and 3.[10] These data characterize the relationship between the occupational category of the father when his son was fourteen years old, and the socio-occupational category of the son at the time the study was carried out.

Outflow

Table 2 shows that the majority of men belong to a socio-occupational category different from that of their fathers. The proportion of mobile individuals fluctuates from 96% for sons of unskilled laborers to 51% for those of skilled workers. The percentage of mobile peasants' sons is very high (75%), with the majority of them entering the category of skilled manual workers. The vast majority of sons of unskilled laborers also enter the category of skilled workers, while the majority of mobile sons of skilled workers go on to perform nonmanual work. In turn, the sons of white-collar workers most often become employed as skilled nonmanual workers, though the proportion in this category that goes over to manual work is also significant, reaching 40% in the case of children of managers.

The main directions of outflow are: from agricultural labor to

Table 2

Mobility from Father's Occupation to Respondent's Occupation: Outflow Percentages for Men Aged 30 to 39 in 1972

Father's occupation[a]	Respondent's occupation													
	(1)	(2)	(3)	(4)	(5)	(6)	(7)	(8)	(9)	(10)	(11)	(12)	Total	N = 100%
(1) Professionals	40.3	6.6	12.3	2.9	2.1	3.7	5.3	20.6	1.2	2.1	2.9	—	100.0	243
(2) Managers	41.7	3.8	7.6	8.3	1.5	3.8	1.5	25.8	1.5	2.3	1.5	0.8	100.0	132
(3) Semi-professionals	35.6	4.8	18.1	4.3	1.6	3.2	3.7	24.5	1.6	1.6	0.5	0.5	100.0	188
(4) Office workers	29.3	2.7	17.4	6.5	2.7	4.9	8.2	22.3	2.2	2.7	—	1.1	100.0	184
(5) Service workers	19.9	2.1	7.8	4.6	3.9	2.8	6.0	38.4	8.2	3.6	1.8	0.7	100.0	281
(6) Owners	13.0	2.8	7.6	3.1	3.5	8.7	8.0	40.4	4.5	3.5	4.3	0.5	100.0	423
(7) Foremen	14.2	3.1	11.1	3.1	1.2	5.6	13.0	44.4	2.5	1.2	—	0.6	100.0	162
(8) Skilled manual workers	14.2	1.8	6.7	2.7	1.7	3.2	9.0	49.3	5.9	3.2	1.2	1.2	100.0	1,482
(9) Semi-skilled manual workers	8.8	1.6	6.0	1.8	3.0	2.3	9.6	49.7	8.7	4.2	2.4	1.9	100.0	737
(10) Unskilled manual workers	8.3	2.0	5.7	2.0	2.3	2.0	10.6	51.9	8.9	3.7	1.4	1.1	100.0	349
(11) Farmers	7.8	1.5	3.7	2.4	2.3	2.3	5.5	33.3	8.1	4.3	25.1	3.8	100.0	4,288
(12) Agricultural laborers	4.8	1.0	2.9	2.6	2.6	1.3	9.3	45.7	8.3	4.5	6.1	11.2	100.0	313
Total	12.1	2.0	5.8	2.7	2.3	2.9	7.0	38.4	7.0	3.8	13.3	2.7	100.0	8,782

[a] Father's occupation when the respondent was 14 years old.

manual work outside of agriculture; from less skilled manual work to more skilled; from manual to nonmanual work; and from less to more skilled nonmanual work. These directions of outflow correspond to intergenerational changes in the occupational structure. As a result of these changes, the process of upward mobility is more common than that of social degradation. Mobile individuals account for 76 percent of the sample studied; of these 61% moved upward in the hierarchy of occupational categories and only 15% moved downward.

Inflow

If we examine inflow into particular occupational categories, we find that respondents of peasant origin are the most numerous (see Table 3). The proportion of respondents of peasant origin varies from 31 percent in the category of professionals to 67 percent in that of agricultural laborers. Ninety-two percent remain in the category of private farmers. Considered together, children of workers and peasants constitute a decisive majority in all groups; in the groups of professionals and managers their proportion is about two-thirds.

Inheritance of fathers' occupation plays a crucial role in the recruitment of individuals to the category of private farmers. In terms of social origin this group is the most homogeneous. Relatively strong homogeneity also characterizes all groups of manual workers, while the category of professionals and semiprofessionals is the most heterogeneous.

Intergroup differences in the structure of outflow and inflow

From our analysis we see that occupational categories of origin differ with respect to occupational destination; the categories of occupational destination differ with respect to social origin. The question arises, therefore, whether the distribution of these differences reflects some more general regularity. An answer may

Table 3

Mobility from Father's Occupation to Respondent's Occupation: Inflow Percentages for Men Aged 30 to 39 in 1972

Father's occupation[a]	Respondent's occupation												
	(1)	(2)	(3)	(4)	(5)	(6)	(7)	(8)	(9)	(10)	(11)	(12)	Total
(1) Professionals	9.2	9.3	5.9	2.9	2.4	3.5	2.1	1.5	0.5	1.5	0.6	—	2.8
(2) Managers	5.2	2.9	2.0	4.6	1.0	2.0	0.3	1.0	0.3	0.9	0.2	0.4	1.5
(3) Semi-professionals	6.3	5.2	6.7	3.3	1.5	2.4	1.1	1.4	0.5	0.9	0.1	0.4	2.1
(4) Office workers	5.1	2.9	6.3	5.0	2.4	3.5	2.4	1.2	0.7	1.5	—	0.8	2.1
(5) Service workers	5.3	3.5	4.3	5.4	5.4	3.1	2.8	3.2	3.8	3.0	0.4	0.8	3.2
(6) Owners	5.2	7.0	6.3	5.4	7.3	14.5	5.5	5.1	3.1	4.5	1.5	0.8	4.8
(7) Foremen	2.2	2.9	3.6	2.1	1.0	3.5	3.4	2.1	0.7	0.6	—	0.4	1.8
(8) Skilled manual workers	19.9	15.1	19.5	16.6	12.2	18.4	21.8	21.7	14.2	14.1	1.5	7.5	16.9
(9) Semi-skilled manual workers	6.1	7.0	8.7	5.4	10.7	6.7	11.5	10.9	10.4	9.3	1.5	5.8	8.4
(10) Unskilled manual workers	2.7	4.1	3.9	2.9	3.9	2.7	6.0	5.4	5.1	3.9	0.4	1.7	4.0
(11) Farmers	31.4	38.4	31.0	43.2	48.3	38.0	38.2	42.4	56.6	55.6	92.0	66.8	48.8
(12) Agricultural laborers	1.4	1.7	1.8	3.3	3.9	1.6	4.7	4.2	4.2	4.2	1.6	14.5	3.6
Total	100.0	100.0	100.0	100.0	100.0	100.0	100.0	100.0	100.0	100.0	100.0	100.0	100.0
N = 100%	1,061	172	507	241	205	255	615	3,371	613	333	1,168	241	8,782

[a]Father's occupation when the respondent was 14 years old.

be sought in terms of both outflow and inflow distributions for each occupational category. The index of dissimilarity (Δ) is a synthetic measure of differences in the structure of outflow and inflow between the two categories.. The value of the index equals the sum of the differences of the same sign in the percentage distribution of compared categories in the table of social mobility. This index value ranges from 0 (full similarity) to 100 (full dissimilarity).

In Table 4 the entries above the main diagonal are the values of the index of dissimilarity for outflows. Thus, for example, the number given in row 1, column 8, characterizes the differences in the current occupational composition of the children of professionals and of skilled workers. The figure indicates that 40% of the children of professionals or skilled workers would have to be transferred in order for the two groups of origin not to differ in terms of current occupational distribution. In contrast, differences in the social origin of current occupational categories are characterized by the indices presented below the main diagonal of Table 4. Generally, the dissimilarity between categories is greater the further from each other they are situated in the mobility table.

Social distance

Social distance can be inferred from the differences between outflow occupational distributions of persons originating in all occupational categories. In order to establish the distance between any pair of occupational categories we applied multidimensional scaling (e.g., Blau and Duncan, 1977; Hauser and Featherman, 1977).

In this study the purpose of employing multidimensional scaling in social mobility tables was to measure the distance between occupational categories, as well as to determine the relations between the scale and indices of inequality in access to various material and nonmaterial goods. The multi-dimensional scaling program MINISSA[11] was applied to the matrix of values of the index of dissimilarity computed on the basis of intergenerational

Table 4

Values of the Index of Dissimilarity among Occupational Groups for Outflow Mobility (above Diagonal) and Inflow Mobility (below Diagonal)[a]

Occupational groups	(1)	(2)	(3)	(4)	(5)	(6)	(7)	(8)	(9)	(10)	(11)	(12)
(1) Professionals	—	13	12	18	31	36	36	40	45	48	48	54
(2) Managers	12	—	14	20	28	35	36	37	45	45	48	53
(3) Semi-professionals	8	13	—	12	29	36	33	38	46	46	48	54
(4) Office workers	14	13	17	—	26	30	28	33	40	41	46	49
(5) Service workers	27	18	24	14	—	13	20	15	18	20	27	26
(6) Owners	18	12	15	15	20	—	14	13	17	19	29	20
(7) Foremen	22	17	17	18	16	15	—	13	20	20	38	29
(8) Skilled manual workers	23	18	20	14	13	17	6	—	8	8	30	20
(9) Semi-skilled manual workers	35	25	31	22	12	28	19	15	—	4	25	14
(10) Unskilled manual workers	31	22	28	18	10	24	18	14	4	—	28	16
(11) Farmers	61	54	61	49	44	54	54	50	36	36	—	25
(12) Agricultural laborers	49	41	49	35	29	42	38	35	21	22	27	—

[a]Computations based on Tables 2 and 3.

Table 5

Coordinates of Occupational Groups Derived from Outflow Mobility[a]

Occupational groups	Two-dimensional solution[b]		One-dimensional solution[c]
	First dimension	Second dimension	
(1) Professionals	−1.300	.193	−1.462
(2) Managers	−1.185	.472	−1.321
(3) Semi-professionals	−1.305	−.093	−1.338
(4) Office workers	−1.051	−.325	−1.075
(5) Service workers	.104	.102	.064
(6) Owners	.310	−.107	.315
(7) Foremen	.185	−.644	.187
(8) Skilled manual workers	.502	−.337	.438
(9) Semi-skilled manual workers	.798	−.110	.745
(10) Unskilled manual workers	.858	−.263	.724
(11) Farmers	.845	1.035	1.527
(12) Agricultural laborers	1.239	.079	1.196

[a]Based on the matrix of intergroup dissimilarities.
[b]Stress coefficient $S = .027$; the variance equals .826 and .174 for first and second dimensions, respectively.
[c]Stress coefficient $S = .107$.

outflows. The standard adopted to match the space configuration obtained with the original matrix of indices of dissimilarity (that is, with the original empirical data) is the Kruskal coefficient (known also as the stress coefficient). The value of this coefficient decreases as we shift from an ordering of subjects in unidimensional space to ordering them in two- or multi-dimensional space. A decrease in the size of the coefficient indicates the improvement in the fit obtained when we introduce an additional dimension.

One- and two-dimensional solutions are given in Table 5. As can be seen from the values of the stress coefficient, the shift from the linear to the two-dimensional solution noticeably (though not by much) improves the matching of configurations obtained with the matrices of empirical indices of dissimilarity.[12]

In the two-dimensional solution the first dimension clearly plays a more important role than the second. It explains about 83

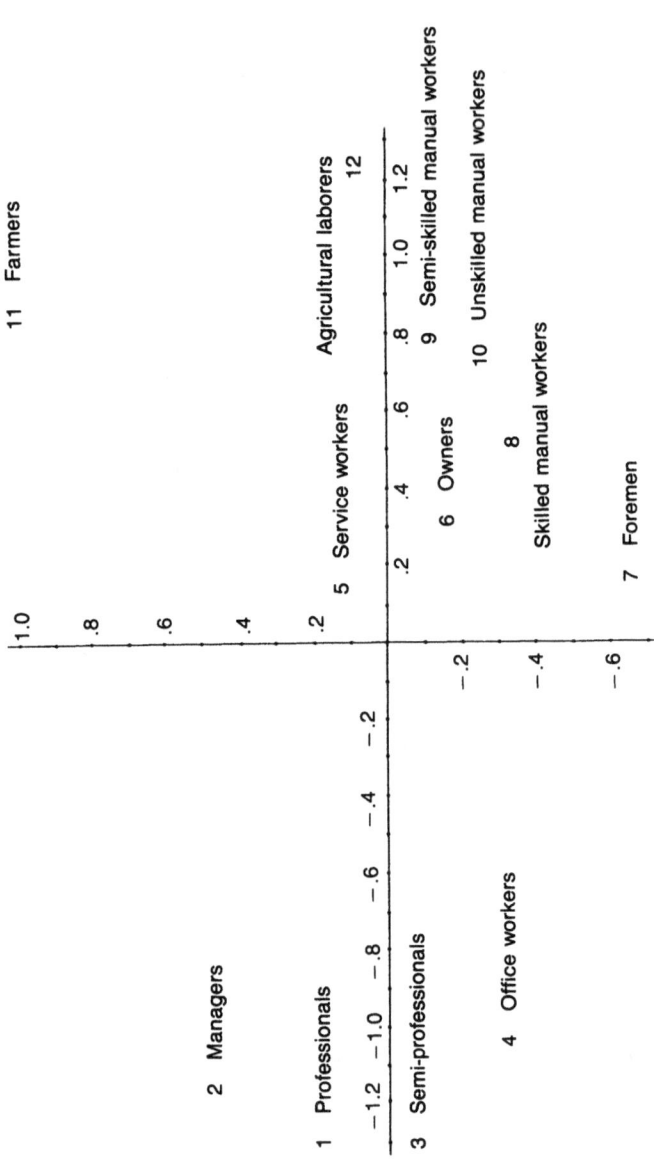

Figure 1. Two dimensional configuration of occupational groups based on multidimensional scaling of dissimilarities between distributions of outflow mobility.

percent of the variance in the outflow of individuals. This dimension is essentially consistent with the hierarchy of occupational categories adopted earlier in the study, and it substantiates its validity on the basis of the analysis of the process of social mobility. Minor disparities generally involve "exchange" of positions in the hierarchy between neighboring groups separated by only a slight distance.

In Table 5 we observe that a great distance separates white- and blue-collar workers along the first dimension: the distance between various categories of white-collar workers is small in comparison to that between them and manual workers. If we accept that this type of discontinuity in the hierarchical structure of groups points to the existence of "class" divisions (Ossowski, 1968: 164-5), then the division into nonmanual and manual workers must be recognized as the crucial one. Among blue-collar workers the group that subsumes the occupations of more highly skilled workers—foremen, artisans, and skilled workers—is rather clearly demarcated from the remaining groups. Low-skilled manual workers and farmers follow, and at the end come agricultural laborers, separated from the rest by some distance.

Along the second dimension only the group of farmers is clearly separated from other occupational categories. Relatively little differentiation exists along this dimension. The small amount of variance that it does explain confirms its quite minor significance. For this reason, a scale with a one-dimensional solution is utilized in the section below.

Social distance and social inequality

The scale constructed on the basis of intergenerational outflows directly measures the distance between occupational categories; the distance reflects how a father's position determines a son's position in the occupational structure. The empirical meaning of this scale is likewise found in its relation to the indices of social inequality—that is, in its correlation with the group characteristics shown in Table 1. The correlation between the scale of social distance and these charateristics is especially strong for education ($r = .97$), the level of standard of living ($.86 \leq r \leq .95$), and power ($.85 \leq r \leq .90$).

Social mobility and social inequality

Given the strong correlation between various aspects of social inequality and social distance based on the analysis of processes of social mobility, the question arises as to how we can best depict the basis of this correlation. What is the common cause for the hierarchical order of broad occupational categories established according to the various criteria considered earlier?

It seems that such a cause may be "power" understood in a broad sense. Parkin (1974: 46) writes: "When we treat power as an aspect of stratification and not simply as differentiation of roles, we cannot easily separate it from material and symbolic elements of inequality. . . . In reality to a certain degree the understanding of stratification in terms of power may be . . . another way of conceptualizing the division of class and status advantages." Under this conceptualization, power is a nonobservable, latent variable which lies at the basis of the distribution of rewards in society. The observable indices describe the extent to which occupational groups participate in obtaining socially desired goods.

The broad understanding of power as a latent variable is not inconsistent with a narrower understanding of it as an attribute of leading positions held in political parties, a state administration, or a nationalized economy. Power narrowly understood can be treated as one of the sources and, simultaneously, as one of the indices of power understood broadly, just as its source may be the ownership of the means of production, education, skills, or other forms of "cultural capital" sought on the labor market.

We can expect that the higher the position of a social group on the scale of power (broadly understood), the more effectively such a group can compete with others not only over goods but, equally, over ensuring for its offspring access to privileged groups. As a result we can expect not only a positive and generally strong correlation among the various goods consumed, but also a strong positive correlation between possession of these goods and the ability of members of social groups to place their children at higher rungs of the social ladder. As we have seen, the latter correlation does actually appear in Polish society and it can, therefore, be viewed as a support for the hypothesis of "social closure." Substantiation of this hypothesis is not total, however. In Poland sons of workers and peasants constitute a majority in all occupational groups, including those most highly placed in the social hierarchy. For this reason we ought to speak not of social closure but rather of "social confinement." This consists of a decrease in the relative opportunities available for children of persons located further down on the social ladder to accede to higher social positions, and the relatively greater opportunities for children of individuals occupying high social positions.

Inequality of opportunity

A classic issue in research on social mobility is the nature of the relationship between social origin and opportunity for achievement. The principle of "equality of opportunity" in access to social positions has traditionally been propagated by liberal-democratic ideologies (for a review see Goldthorpe, 1980), but during the last decade it has also been advanced as an essential goal of social policy in socialist countries (e.g. Pajestka, 1975: 290-7).

To evaluate the chances for mobility on the part of members of particular social groups, use was made of measures based on a multiplicative model of the mobility table proposed by Hauser (1978, 1980). This model is a modified version of Goodman's (1972), dealing with data in a contingency table.

Hauser (1978, 1980) suggests computing the mobility ratio R^*_{ij} for all cells of a mobility table as a measure of the tendency toward mobility (or immobility when $i = j$) (see also Featherman and Hauser, 1978: 156-7). A ratio equalling 1 indicates that in a

Table 6

Design Matrix for a Multiplicative Model with Twelve Levels of Interaction

	Respondent's occupation											
Father's occupation	(1)	(2)	(3)	(4)	(5)	(6)	(7)	(8)	(9)	(10)	(11)	(12)
(1) Professionals	2	2	3	4	5	4	5	7	11	8	4	11
(2) Managers	3	5	7	3	9	6	12	10	12	8	10	10
(3) Semi-professionals	3	4	4	5	9	7	10	9	12	10	12	11
(4) Office workers	4	6	4	4	6	5	6	10	11	8	11	8
(5) Service workers	5	7	7	5	5	8	8	7	7	8	9	10
(6) Owners	8	6	8	7	6	4	7	8	10	8	5	11
(7) Foremen	8	6	6	8	11	6	6	8	12	8	11	11
(8) Skilled manual workers	8	9	9	8	9	8	7	7	9	8	11	8
(9) Semi-skilled manual workers	10	9	9	10	7	9	7	7	8	7	8	6
(10) Unskilled manual workers	8	9	8	9	9	8	6	7	8	6	11	10
(11) Farmers	9	8	10	8	7	8	8	8	7	8	1	3
(12) Agricultural laborers	11	10	11	8	7	11	6	7	7	7	4	1

given subgroup mobility is no different from what we would expect as a result of three effects—scale, row, and column. These are effects of sample size and of origin and destination distributions. A ratio greater or smaller than one indicates that an "interaction"—that is, a tendency toward mobility or immobility—occurs, as a result of the impact of the three effects mentioned above.

Using mobility ratios we can compare the relative chances of mobility for various sets of cells in a mobility table independent of the influence of origin and destination. The model reflects the idea of conditional independence: within a selected set of cells with a given level of interaction, destination is independent of origin.

To design a model for a given mobility table it is necessary to distinguish some sets of cells characterized by the same level of interaction (Table 6). This decision may follow from social theory (see Goldthorpe, 1980) or it may be based on trial and error. The empirical criterion of fitting the model to the data is based on the test of goodness of fit.

In constructing the model, the method of trial and error was used. Accordingly, the model is explanatory rather than confirmatory. Table 7 presents mobility ratios based on the multiplicative model of Hauser.[13] The configuration of mobility ratios in Table 7 indicates the strong tendency toward immobility for the extreme occupational groups. For example, the probability that sons of farmers or agricultural laborers will remain in their father's occupational group is 10 to 11 times greater than the analogous chances for sons of skilled and semiskilled workers. Obviously, there are different reasons for the stability encountered at the bottom and at the top of the occupational hierarchy. At one end limited access to cultural and material goods and a consequent deficiency in "bases of mobility" makes social advancement difficult; at the other the same bases make it possible to retain achieved social position.

The values of mobility ratios demonstrate the tendency toward greater exchange among categories of nonmanual workers, and

Table 7

Mobility Ratios of a Multiplicative Model with Twelve Levels of Interaction

Father's occupation	Respondent's occupation											
	(1)	(2)	(3)	(4)	(5)	(6)	(7)	(8)	(9)	(10)	(11)	(12)
(1) Professionals	6.96	7.32	3.60	2.32	1.95	2.80	1.72	1.14	0.34	1.09	2.54	—
(2) Managers	3.35	1.97	1.03	3.13	0.68	1.34	0.23	0.66	0.20	0.56	0.62	0.66
(3) Semi-professionals	3.22	2.80	2.77	1.80	0.80	1.27	0.63	0.71	0.23	0.45	0.25	0.52
(4) Office workers	2.61	1.57	2.61	2.69	1.34	1.92	1.35	0.64	0.31	0.74	—	1.04
(5) Service workers	1.75	1.21	1.16	1.90	1.92	1.09	0.99	1.08	1.16	0.96	0.80	0.67
(6) Owners	0.97	1.36	0.95	1.06	1.46	2.86	1.12	0.97	0.54	0.81	1.62	0.38
(7) Foremen	0.94	1.32	1.25	0.95	0.45	1.62	1.60	0.94	0.26	0.25	—	0.44
(8) Skilled manual workers	0.99	0.80	0.79	0.88	0.65	0.97	1.17	1.11	0.66	0.68	0.43	0.91
(9) Semi-skilled manual workers	0.61	0.73	0.70	0.57	1.15	0.71	1.25	1.12	0.97	0.90	0.87	1.42
(10) Unskilled manual workers	0.58	0.91	0.68	0.66	0.89	0.62	1.38	1.17	0.96	0.80	0.51	0.86
(11) Farmers	0.69	0.89	0.55	0.96	1.14	0.88	0.91	0.95	1.15	1.17	11.36	3.60
(12) Agricultural laborers	0.39	0.50	0.40	0.97	1.15	0.45	1.41	1.20	1.08	1.12	2.51	9.78

toward significant limitations on such exchange between them and the remaining categories. The line between nonmanual workers and the remaining categories is indicated by the fall in the values of mobility ratios. Generally the mobility ratios characterizing exchange between the four categories of white-collar workers and categories of service workers, owners of artisan workshops, and foremen are greater than 1. Also evident is the tendency toward relatively intensive exchange between both categories of agricultural occupations—private farmers and hired laborers—and a significant limitation in their exchange with other categories. As a rule the indices of mobility between white- and blue-collar workers are lower than 1.

The correlation between relative chances for mobility and social distance between occupational groups is negative: indices of mobility become smaller as distance between compared groups becomes larger. Exceptions to this regularity are related to the small size of many of the 144 cells in the mobility table.

Relative chances for access to particular social groups differ markedly according to social origin. For example, compared with the sons of skilled workers, the sons of professionals have more than a seven times greater chance of attaining a professional position than those of the skilled workers' category. Compared with the sons of agricultural laborers, the sons of professionals have an eighteen times greater chance of attaining a position in the intelligentsia. Similarly, compared with children of the intelligentsia, children of workers have unfavorable chances of obtaining a managerial position.

This differentiation of relative opportunities in access to high social position—far removed from the principle of "equality of opportunity"—is a reflection of the rigidity of the social structure, not only in terms of the flows between the top and the bottom of the hierarchy but also of flows between the extremes and center of the hierarchy. For example, children of subordinate office personnel have a nearly three times greater relative chance of attaining a professional position than have children of skilled workers.

If the large-scale process of social mobility permits many members of society to change social position in comparison to their father's (and generally to achieve social advancement), the position attained in this process still depends in great measure on social origin. The composition of social groups that have been "nominated"—that is, created as a result of the application of individual criteria of selection—is also shaped by collective group criteria, in particular, social origin. Origin also indirectly influences the composition of nominated groups by affecting such criteria of selection as education[14] or, in the case of directors and managers, party membership.

Notes

1. Marx gave little consideration to the issue of social mobility, although, as many sociologists concerned with social stratification emphasize today, he was aware of the significant implications that social mobility had for the formation of social classes and the creation of class consciousness. This is most clearly evident in the Marxian analysis of class relations in American society (see Goldthorpe, 1980: chapter 1).

2. This conception was modified and considerably developed by Parkin (1979).

3. Both mechanisms also appear in contemporary capitalist countries although the market mechanism plays the decisive role (Parkin, 1974).

4. The term "social group" is used here in a broad sense. Such an approach, according to Ossowski, "permits us to treat every collectivity of individuals as a social group if the researcher or observer perceives sufficiently important relations between them for his conceptual framework. . . . From the viewpoint of the observer such a concept of social group means that a collectivity of people can constitute a group even though its members may not perceive any links between them in exactly such dimensions" (1962: 81). To avoid repetition, the terms "occupational group" and "occupational category" are used interchangeably.

5. "Principal job" is understood as the respondent's work which takes up the relatively greatest amount of his time. "Income from principal job" includes basic pay; monthly, quarterly and yearly bonuses; awards; the monetary value of the main goods purchased at an employees' discount; and remuneration for overtime at an employee's main place of work.

6. Strictly speaking, we are concerned with the average income per person in a household; in practice this is generally a family.

7. The level of income corresponding to the social minimum is that identified by Tymowski (1973). Some critics argue that this level is rather low. Accordingly, the percent of individuals living below the social minimum that is

given here should be treated as a minimum estimate.

8. Permanent employees of the party apparatus who are politically active have been included in the group of "managers."

9. It is possible, of course, to treat membership in the PUWP as an index of real sharing in power to the degree that such members can influence matters at their work place, neighborhood and so on by participating in the work party organizational units.

10. Given constraints of space, data on the social mobility of women have been excluded. Comparative aspects of the process of socio-occupational achievement for men and women in Poland were examined in a separate study (Pohoski 1979).

11. The version of the program GKLR MINISSA-1 corrected by E. E. Roskam and J. C. Lingoes was used.

12. There is no strictly determined level below which one can recognize the value of the Kruskal coefficient as indicating a good representation of empirical data. By convention the value 0.10 has been employed. A small decrease of this value brought about by the inclusion of an additional dimension shows that adding a new dimension is unproductive (MacDonald, 1972: 214–15; Kruskal, 1964a, 1964b).

13. I am grateful to Professor Robert Hauser of the University of Wisconsin for the computer program and instruction in its use.

14. The type of "school career" clearly depends on social origin: for example, only 9% of the sons who had an intelligentsia background ended their school careers with elementary school, and 36% went on to attain university education; the respective figures for sons of skilled workers were 32% and 10%, and for sons of farmers 62% and 5%. In turn, the type of school career determines to a great degree the type of occupational career (Pohoski, 1984).

References

Blau, P. M. and O. D. Duncan
    1967   *The American Occupational Structure*. New York: Wiley.
Davis, K. and W. E. Moore
    1945   "Some principles of stratification." *American Sociological Review* 10:242–9.
Featherman, D. L. and R. M. Hauser
    1978   *Opportunity and Change*. New York: Academic Press.
Giddens, A.
    1973   *The Class Structure of the Advanced Societies*. London: Hutchinson.
Goldthorpe, J. H.
    1980   *Social Mobility and Class Structure in Modern Britain*. Oxford: Clarendon Press.
Hauser, R. M.
    1980   "Some exploratory methods for modeling mobility tables and other cross-classified data." Pp. 413–58 in K. F. Schuessler

(ed.), *Sociological Methodology*. San Francisco: Jossey-Bass.
1978 "A structural model of the mobility table." *Social Forces* 56:919–53.

Hauser, R. M. and D. L. Featherman
1977 *The Process of Social Stratification*. New York: Academic Press.

Jaźwińska-Motylska, E.
1982 Ruchliwość społeczno-zawodowa mieszkańców Warszawy. [Socio-occupational Mobility of the Inhabitants of Warsaw.] Unpublished Ph.D. dissertation, University of Warsaw.

Kłoskowska, A.
1981 *Socjologia kultury*. [The Sociology of Culture.] Warsaw: Polish Scientific Publishers.

Kruskal, J. B.
1964a "Multidimensional scaling by optimizing goodness of fit to a nonmetric hypothesis." *Psychometrika* 29:1–27.
1964b "Nonmetric multidimensional scaling: a numerical method." *Psychometrika* 29:115–29.

Lissowski, G.
1976 "Ocena reprezentatywności próby do badań nad ruchliwością społeczno-zawodową" [Evaluation of the representativeness of the sample in research on socio-occupational mobility]. In M. Pohoski (ed.), *Ruchliwość społeczna w procesie rozwoju gospodarczego*. [Social Mobility in the Process of Economic Development.] Vol. 1. The Institute of Sociology of the University of Warsaw. Mimeo.

MacDonald, K. I.
1972 "MDSCAL and distances between socioeconomic groups." Pp. 211–34 in K. Hope (ed.), *The Analysis of Social Mobility. Methods and Approaches*. Oxford: Oxford University Press.

Maslow, A.
1943 "A theory of human motivation." *Psychological Review* 50:370–96.

Narojek, W.
1973 *Społeczeństwo planujące*. [The Planning Society.] Warsaw: Polish Scientific Publishers.

Ossowski, S.
1968 *Dzieła*. [Collected Works.] Vol. 5. Warsaw: Polish Scientific Publishers.
1962 *O osobliwościach nauk społecznych*. [On Peculiarities of Social Sciences.] Warsaw: Polish Scientific Publishers.

Pajestka, J.
1975 *Determinanty postępu*. [Determinants of Progress] Warsaw: Polish Economic Publishers.

Parkin, F.
1979 *Marxism and Class Theory: A Bourgeois Critique*. New York: Columbia University Press.

1974 "Strategies of social closure in class formation." In: F. Parkin (ed.), *The Social Analysis of Class Structure*. London: Tavistock Publications.
1971 *Class Inequality and Political Order*. New York: Praeger.
Pohoski, M.
    1984 *Ruchliwość społeczna w Polsce*. [Social Mobility in Poland.] In press.
    1979 "Proces osiągnięć społeczno-zawodowych w Polsce" [The process of socio-occupational attainment in Poland]. In: *Tendencje rozwoju społecznego*. [Trends in Social Development.] Warsaw: Central Statistical Office.
Pohoski, M. and K. M. Słomczyński
    1978 *Społeczna klasyfikacja zawodów*. [Social Classification of Occupations.] Warsaw: The Institute of Philosophy and Sociology of the Polish Academy of Sciences.
Słomczyński, K. M. and G. Kacprowicz
    1979 *Skale zawodów*. [Scales of Occupations.] Warsaw: The Institute of Philosophy and Sociology of the Polish Academy of Sciences.
Tymowski, A.
    1973 *Minimum socjalne*. [The Social Minimum.] Warsaw: Polish Scientific Publishers.
Wasilewski, J.
    1981 *Kariery społeczno-zawodowe dyrektorów*. [Socio-occupational Careers of Managers.] Wrocław: Ossolineum.
Wesołowski, W.
    1975 *Teoria, badania, praktyka*. [Theory, Research, Practice.] Warsaw: Książka i Wiedza.

Changes in Social Structure and in How It Is Popularly Perceived

KRYSTYNA JANICKA

Introduction

The research discussed in this paper was conducted in the city of Łódź in four separate surveys in 1965, 1967, 1976, and 1980. Each time, a randomly selected sample of working men aged 21 to 65, heads of families, was interviewed. The sizes of the samples were 1,000, 1,000, 960, and 975 in the respective years. The most recent survey was conducted in November-December 1980. Like its predecessors, it is part of a series of studies on social differentiation among the urban population.

Occupational differentiation is an important focus of this series. The systematic use of a typology of occupational categories allows one to analyze Poland's social structure in its three different dimensions: class, gradational, and functional (Ossowski, 1963). White-collar and blue-collar workers are distinguished according to the content of their work; these groups are directly related to the social classes of an urban population: the intelligentsia and the working class. The gradational dimension is based on

---

This survey research project was initiated by Włodzimierz Wesołowski. The first surveys, conducted in 1965 and 1967, were administered by the Department of Sociology of Łódź University. In 1976 and 1980 the research was supported by and carried out under the auspices of the Institute of Philosophy and Sociology, the Polish Academy of Sciences. Several books based on this research have been published: Wesołowski (1970); Słomczyński and Wesołowski (1973); Słomczyński (1972); Warzywoda-Kruszyńska (1974); Janicka (1976); Kobus-Wojciechowska (1977).

the criteria of occupational skills and educational requirements. In turn, the functional dimension corresponds to the type of work performed and the branch and sector of the economy. The interrelationships of these three dimensions become clear when the task of aggregating individual occupations into occupational groups is undertaken. In this study we are concerned with the following occupational groups: (1) professionals; (2) technicians; (3) office workers; (4) foremen; (5) service workers; (6) skilled workers; (7) semiskilled workers; and (8) unskilled laborers.[1]

Understanding social structure in terms of occupational categories certainly does not exhaust the list of possible conceptualizations. However, ours retains substantive importance given the inevitability of the division of labor in a society and the consequences for individuals of performing occupational roles. In successive studies the project took into account the problem of social differentiation on several basic dimensions, including those concerned with social consciousness. Two aspects of occupational differentiation in which the objective state of affairs can be contrasted with subjective feelings about them are considered here: income from work and housing conditions of the whole family. In addition, later sections of this paper discuss (1) perceptions of social class, strata, and groups; (2) feelings about the degree to which the kind of work performed, size of income, level of education, and extent of power engender conflict; and (3) egalitarian attitudes toward income distribution.

Differentiation in the standard of living: Facts and perceptions

In analyses dealing with self-evaluation of social status and with the image of social divisions and the perception of sources of social conflicts, a centrally important factor is the standard of living, which is associated with personal income. In the second half of the 1970s various attempts were made to synthesize long-term economic changes; findings indicated growing inequality in income distribution. The discontent and social tensions that were

Table 1

Occupational Groups and Monthly Earnings (Łódź, 1967, 1976, 1980)

Occupational group and year		Arithmetic mean in zlotys	Rate of change	Coefficient of variability[a]	Ratio to lowest earnings
Professionals	1967	3,419	100	.25	198
	1976	6,021	176	.38	193
	1980	7,728	128	.36	160
Technicians	1967	2,681	100	.19	155
	1976	4,434	165	.26	142
	1980	6,045	136	.27	125
Office workers	1967	2,258	100	.19	138
	1976	4,780	212	.32	153
	1980	6,350	133	.24	132
Foremen	1967	2,378	100	.19	131
	1976	4,429	186	.19	142
	1980	6,805	154	.22	141
Service workers	1967	1,924	100	.25	112
	1976	3,923	204	.28	126
	1980	5,859	149	.24	121
Skilled workers	1967	2,056	100	.19	119
	1976	3,911	190	.23	125
	1980	5,859	149	.23	121
Semi-skilled workers	1967	1,851	100	.12	107
	1976	3,585	194	.24	115
	1980	5,403	151	.21	112
Unskilled workers	1967	1,722	100	.19	100
	1976	3,117	181	.24	100
	1980	4,821	155	.26	100

[a]Ratio of standard deviation to the mean.

created attracted attention and eventually produced the massive upheavals of August 1980. Accordingly, it is important to ask to what extent various socio-occupational groups differ with respect to standard of living, and whether the distribution of income and access to basic goods was very different in 1980 compared to previous years.

A comparison of the average monthly income in 1976 and 1980

indicates that basic wages of unskilled workers and foremen increased the most (155% and 154% when the 1976 basic salary is treated as 100%). By contrast, professionals and office workers received the smallest increase in monthly wages (see Table 1).

Compared to the period 1967-76, the rate of increase of wages in the period 1976-80 is, on the whole, lower and more even. There was a reduction in the disparity between the wages of clearly polarized groups—professionals and unskilled workers. In 1967 the top wages were on average 198 percent higher than the minimum, while in 1976 the corresponding figure fell slightly, to 193, and four years later, in 1980, it had decreased to 160. We can speak, therefore, of a systematic reduction in intergroup disparity in terms of basic wages. Moreover, the values of the variability coefficients of intragroup differentiation did not increase.

A certain incongruence can be detected, however, between the growth in wages and the declining proportion of people who experienced an improvement in their standard of living during the last decade (see Table 2). We can assume that consumer aspirations, which continued to increase in the second half of the 1970s, had an important effect on people's feelings about economic standing. In 1976, from 62 to nearly 90 percent of respondents (depending on their occupational category) affirmed that they had felt an improvement in their economic conditions during the last decade. With the exception of the lowest-skilled workers, this proportion fell markedly in 1980. The greatest decrease occurred among skilled workers and professionals (27.4 and 23.5 percent respectively). Even then, however, at least half of the respondents in each occupational category reported an improvement in their standing. Over 40 percent of this group sensed that the improvement had occurred in the three years immediately preceding the research, that is, between 1978 and 1980. We do not have data that could directly explain the reasons for this evaluation. We conjecture, though, that earlier accumulation of savings, perhaps over the course of several years, permitted respondents to increase their purchasing power in precisely this period.

Table 2

Subjective Evaluation of Change in the Standard of Living during the Past Decade by Occupational Groups (Łódź, 1965, 1976, 1980)[a]

Occupational group	Percent of respondents stating that their standard of living					
	improved slightly or markedly			worsened slightly or markedly		
	1965	1976	1980	1965	1976	1980
Professionals	42.9	79.7	56.2	22.0	2.5	16.3
Technicians	37.9	77.5	60.9	17.2	4.2	14.9
Office workers	30.1	80.5	66.7	16.1	6.1	13.9
Foremen	22.8	87.6	74.3	29.1	2.8	5.9
Service workers	20.5	80.6	59.1	27.0	7.1	10.0
Skilled workers	25.4	79.8	52.4	29.7	5.7	14.1
Semi-skilled workers	23.7	72.7	63.3	25.5	10.9	16.7
Unskilled workers	25.6	62.7	67.6	26.7	10.4	8.8

[a] In 1965 respondents were asked to evaluate changes in their standard of living "in recent years," not "during the past decade." For the three surveys the answers "no change" and "no opinion" are omitted.

Table 3 presents data on housing conditions and juxtaposes them with respondents' evaluations. We note that after a distinct improvement had been recorded between 1965 and 1976 in the average number of persons occupying a room, stagnation and even a certain deterioration followed. In terms of occupants per room the two extreme groups invariably are the professionals on the one hand and unskilled workers on the other. The disparity in their respective housing conditions was aggravated, however, in the period 1976–80, rising from 0.5 to 0.7. This took place in contrast to a clear egalitarian trend between 1965 and 1976.

Despite increasing difficulties and restrictions affecting the improvement of housing conditions, the percentage of nonmanual workers assessing these conditions as very good or good remained constant from 1976 to 1980. Over all, the percentage ranged from 50 for the unskilled workers to 80 for professionals (see Table 3). Among workers in general, regardless of the level of their skills, there is a drop of approximately 10 percent in

Table 3

Housing Conditions and Subjective Evaluation of Changes in Them by Occupational Groups (Łódź, 1965, 1976, 1980)

Occupational group	Average number of persons per room			Percent of respondents stating that				Improvement occurred between 1976 and 1980[a]
				Their housing conditions are very good or good		Improvement occurred in last decade		
	1965	1976	1980	1976	1980	1976	1980	
Professionals	1.3	1.0	0.9	79	80	48	45	61
Technicians	1.6	1.2	1.1	68	69	52	46	43
Office workers	1.7	1.1	1.2	76	78	48	42	60
Foremen	1.7	1.2	1.2	75	73	57	43	42
Service workers	1.9	1.3	1.3	63	66	47	44	63
Skilled workers	2.1	1.3	1.4	66	55	45	37	57
Semi-skilled workers	2.2	1.2	1.5	64	53	54	37	64
Unskilled workers	2.4	1.5	1.6	57	50	39	35	75

[a]The percent base is the total of those whose housing conditions improved during the past decade.

positive evaluations given. Since the correlation between housing conditions and their subjective assessment is weak, this result can be seen as a symptom of the growing discontent within the working class.

A certain proportion of respondents believed that over the last decade (that is, between 1970 and 1980) an improvement had taken place in their housing conditions; this ranged from 35 percent of unskilled workers to 46 percent of technicians. The majority of those who stated that their housing problems had eased during the past decade felt that the improvement took place between 1976 and 1980. The fact that an evaluation of the period 1976–80 in terms of improvement in housing conditions was no worse than that given in 1976 for the previous five-year period seems to be an effect of the specific situation in Łódź. Around 1975 a major program of reconstruction and development was launched in the city. Another point is, however, that in evaluating housing conditions the most important criterion used may be real personal experience and the awareness of other people's housing situations. Reference groups may serve to moderate one's aspirations.

The perception of social differentiation

In analyzing the everday perception of social structure in our Łódź studies, there were two basic research themes. The first was related to the social groups, strata, and classes, distinguished by individuals, and how relations between these collectivities were perceived. The second theme was linked to the evaluation of social differences between people according to predetermined criteria.[2]

We shall analyze in some detail answers to two open-ended questions: (1) "In your opinion, are the people of this city divided into some social groups, strata, or classes?" and (2) "If so, what are these groups?" The first question deliberately includes the three terms "groups," "strata," and "classes" in order not to reduce the number of affirmative answers, which might have resulted had we imposed a terminology that conceived of social divisions in a strict way. If we had only included the term "class," for example, it might well have had the effect of decreasing the proportion of positive statements, for in Poland the term is frequently used by the mass media to denote the "working class" as distinct from the "intelligentsia." In formulating our questions we wished to offer respondents the opportunity to put forward views that conceived the social structure in other ways; hence the terms "strata" and "groups" were included. It appears that this last term has the broadest meaning in everyday language and essentially is associated with collectivities distinguished by a large set of selected criteria (Słomczyński and Wesołowski, 1973: 243).

The feeling that readily distinguishable social classes, strata, or groups exist in Poland is widespread and has not changed much over time. In both 1965 and 1976 about two-thirds of the respondents perceived social divisions. Four years later, in 1980, perceptions of such divisions were somewhat more widespread. When we aggregated opinions on this subject we found that 80 percent of the population questioned confirmed the existence of various divisions in the social structure. Among professionals and technicians this proportion reached 90 percent.

In recent years a change has occurred in the certainty with which respondents affirm the existence of social divisions. In 1980 sixty percent of respondents expressed the belief that society is *very* clearly divided, an increase of 15 percent compared to 1976. Apart from lower-skilled workers, who referred less often to marked divisions among people in the city, this opinion is equally widespread across various occupational categories.

A comparison of 1965 and 1976 data indicates that the general perception of social structure remained unchanged. This is shown by the relatively constant proportion of various social divisions identified by the respondents. Let us look more closely at this typology of social-structure images (see also: Słomczyński and Wesołowski, 1973: 244–5).

The first type involves class divisions as well as divisions

Table 4

Perceptions of the Bases of Social Differentiation (Łódź, 1965, 1976, 1980)

Type of divisions	Percent of respondents indicating a given type of division[a]		
	1965	1976	1980
(1) Class divisions			
dichotomy: working class—intelligentsia	19.3	18.5	11.6
trichotomy: working class—intelligentsia—private entrepreneurs	13.6	10.8	11.5
based on nature of work	9.4	12.3	10.4
(2) Strata divisions			
education	10.2	12.1	6.3
income	13.2	12.2	18.3
power	9.1	8.1	20.3
life-style	3.2	1.3	1.6
(3) Divisions based on personality traits	3.2	9.2	5.6
Total	N = 1,000	N = 960	N = 975

[a]Respondents could identify more than one type of division.

produced by the nature of work performed; both are connected with the distinctions found in Marxist theory and ideology. In the Marxist conception, class is understood as a historically shaped collectivity, internally differentiated by the relation to the means of production and by the position occupied in the process of production. These, in turn, have consequences for life conditions, social consciousness, and political behavior. In this respect the working class, the intelligentsia, and small-commodity producers represent the basic pillars of the class system of the urban segment of Polish society.

About 30 to 40 percent of respondents tended to accept such a differentiation. The majority identified only the first two classes, the working class and the intelligentsia, and frequently designated the specific occupational categories believed to belong to each. A small percentage also proposed a threefold division, identifying a residual category of "all others." We can assume that had the respondents been more precise they would have referred to small-commodity producers more frequently. The conception of a three-class scheme is inextricably linked with the nature of work performed, especially with the division between manual and nonmanual workers employed by the state, and self-employment. Respondents made quite frequent mention of, on the one hand, "manual and nonmanual workers" and, on the other, "employed people and private entrepreneurs." Other criteria of class division were also used as in statements asserting the existence of a "red bourgeoisie," a "ruling elite," the "proprietors of People's Poland," and the like. These statements, involving political criteria, were made much more often in 1980 than in 1965 or 1976.

The second type of social-structure images entails division by social strata, i.e., a vertical differentiation of society produced by unequal distribution of income, education, and power. These three factors were most frequently identified by respondents. The most general characteristic of their responses was a narrower conceptualization of social stratification than that adopted by sociologists. For example, respondents did not specifically mention life-style but rather differences between "cultured and uncultured persons" or "better- and worse-mannered individuals." The more specific distinctions regarding life-style were usually linked with other social stratification criteria—for example prestige.

In total over one-third of the respondents referred to social-stratification divisions. Whereas in 1965 and 1976 the criteria of income and education, frequently linked to power or life-style, were invoked to an overwhelming degree, by 1980 power and income were perceived as dominating not only strata divisions but class divisions as well. It may be possible that in social consciousness both power and income were seen as performing the role of class divisions.

The third type of perception of social divisions does not refer to structured social inequality but is connected instead with differentiation of personality traits. This type represents a residual category accounting for from 3.2 to 9.2 percent of respondents.

In our analysis of answers to the question about the existence of friction or distrust among the various groups identified by respondents, we find that over half of those responding in 1980 gave a more or less decisive affirmative answer (56%). The extent of perceived distrust within society increased by 14 percent over 1976. What is noteworthy here, as in the case of perceptions of social divisions, is the significant increase in the proportion of decisive responses. In 1976 23.6 percent of respondents perceived friction or distrust between identified groups; in 1980 this figure rose to 40.6 percent.

In successive studies the sense of the conflict-engendering role played by social divisions was shared by ever larger proportions of all occupational categories. In 1965 it ranged from 25 to 36.5 percent, in 1976 from 33 to 45.4 percent, and in 1980 from 46.7 to 80.6 percent. Likewise in 1980, as in 1965 and 1976, the proportion of respondents asserting the existence of intergroup friction in society was no different among various occupational categories than among those that were the result of differentiated sharing in various goods. In 1980 the largest percent of persons affirming that intergroup friction existed was recorded among office workers (80.6%). Among professionals, technicians, and skilled workers this proportion hovered between 50 and 60 percent. In contrast, among less-skilled workers it turned out to be lowest (about 47%).

The sense of the conflict-engendering role played by the basic factors of social differentiation

The questionnaire used in the Łódź studies of 1967, 1976, and 1980 included four items bearing directly on the sense that selected factors of social differentiation played a conflict-engendering role. The first of these questions read: "Do you believe that at present differences in manual and nonmanual work in our country produce conflict between people?" The next three questions were formulated analogously, with "income," "education," and "power" substituted for "manual and nonmanual work." The interpretation of the criteria of social differentiation was left to the respondents. It was assumed that respondents' interpretations are related to meaningful spheres of their everyday observations and experience.

On the basis of information collected from the three surveys we can see that a change in social consciousness occurred in the period 1967–80 (see Table 5). The following conclusion was drawn earlier, from the Łódź research of 1967 and 1976:

> In 1967 a conflict-engendering role was ascribed most often to such factors as income (53%) and education (52%). These were followed by the nature of work (48%) and power (46%). Differences between the relative frequency with which people expressed the view that particular factors generate conflicts can be regarded as minor. The prevalence of factors changed over the course of the next decade. The feeling that both power and the nature of work played a conflict-engendering role was not only less prevalent but both factors had decreased by an almost equal percentage from 1965 to 1976. However, the differences between factors became greater in the cases of education and income. In 1976 fewer respondents cited the conflict-engendering role of education (32.2% compared to 51.7% earlier), but more referred to the analogous role performed by income (68.5% compared to 52.9% earlier). In 1976 income had decisively become the most commonly perceived source of conflicts. (Słomczyński and Wesołowski 1977: 19)

Four years later, in 1980, three of the factors under consideration were thought by respondents to have exacerbated their conflict-engendering role. These were nature of work, income, and power. Income continued to be the most commonly perceived source of social conflict (85% of responses). However, in 1980 power was cited by an only slightly lower proportion of respondents (about 80%), and was mentioned nearly twice as often as in 1976. Thus, in 1980 income and power were perceived as two dimensions of social differentiation along which

Table 5

The Sense of the Conflict-engendering Role Played by Social Differences in Nature of Work, Income, Education, and Power (Łódź, 1967, 1976, 1980)

		Percent of respondents stating that differences							
		currently do not create conflict			currently create conflict				
			10 years ago				10 years ago conflict was		
Differences	Year of research	Total	did not create conflict	created conflict	Total	greater	the same	smaller
Nature of work	1967[a]	51.5	—	—	47.6	—	—	—
	1976	56.6	25.4	29.4	43.1	15.4	13.6	13.2
	1980	38.1	25.9	9.8	60.3	9.4	20.9	27.4
Income	1967[a]	45.5	—	—	52.9	—	—	—
	1976	30.7	15.6	14.7	68.5	15.0	31.1	31.3
	1980	14.2	9.6	2.9	84.9	7.1	27.9	46.8
Education	1967[a]	45.1	—	—	51.7	—	—	—
	1976	66.7	40.6	24.3	32.2	7.5	12.4	11.8
	1980	66.1	51.4	11.5	32.7	4.1	12.7	14.9
Power	1967[a]	46.5	—	—	45.7	—	—	—
	1976	57.5	37.2	18.9	41.4	9.0	20.9	10.7
	1980	17.3	13.4	2.4	79.5	5.5	29.9	39.5

[a]The 1967 survey did not include questions about social conflict ten years earlier.

basic social tensions could be crystallized.

Education, which has always been held in high esteem in Polish society, was mentioned relatively infrequently as a factor producing conflict (by one-third of respondents). The question arises, therefore, why people fail to appreciate that it is precisely education that constitutes the basic factor determining the distribution of rewards. We calculated the correlation between education on the one hand and wages, standard of living, cultural participation, and occupational prestige on the other. The results indicate that between 1965 and 1980 the correlation of education with other elements of social position did not increase. With regard to wages this correlation actually weakened significantly ($r = 0.41$ and 0.32). The only strong, constant correlation remained between education and occupational prestige ($r = 0.76$).

An explanation for the increase in the frequency with which income was deemed by respondents to play a conflict-engendering role can be based on increasing aspirations with respect to consumption. Because of disequilibrium between supply and demand, the chances of fulfilling consumer aspirations became more and more uncertain. A widespread belief existed in 1980 that many goods could be acquired either through a system of personal favors or through substantial overpayment when compared to official prices. Given the inadequate supply of food and durables, the position of groups more favorably situated was felt to be particularly irritating.

The increase in the significance of power as a conflict-engendering factor mirrors the changes in Poland's political system between 1976 and 1980. The authoritarian style of the governmental decision-making process and the growing privileges enjoyed by the ruling elite are examples of these changes, which were linked in social consciousness not only with political power but, speaking more generally, with almost all activities of the government.

Apart from the question concerned with the conflict-engendering role of certain factors, the 1976 and 1980 Łódź questionnaires also asked respondents for an assessment of the conflict-engendering role played by the same factors ten years earlier.[3] The resulting response patterns suggest the existence of distinctive tendencies in the retrospective perception of social reality, as well as distinct modes for its reconstruction.

The majority of respondents who in 1980 did not perceive the sources of conflict as being rooted in income and power tended to support the view that ten years earlier these factors were similarly not responsible for social conflicts. By contrast, those who assigned a conflict-engendering role to particular factors believed overwhelmingly that ten years earlier social conflicts had also been closely related to the same factors. The pattern described is typical not only of 1980 but also of the survey conducted four years earlier.

Egalitarian attitudes toward income distribution

A newly introduced set of issues in the 1980 survey includes opinions concerning recommended levels of earnings, acceptance of wage disparities, access to privileges by certain occupational groups, and criteria that should be used in determining the size of income and evaluating the actual principles of income distribution. In this section we describe the most important response pattern to one question: "Would you support a policy at the present time to decrease the income of persons earning the most, even if this did not lead to an increase in the wages of those earning least?" A four-point scale was employed to measure responses: (a) decidedly yes; (b) on the whole, yes; (c) on the whole, no; (d) decidedly no.

Nearly half the respondents were decisively in favor of a policy reducing the income of the highest earners even if this would not affect the wage level of the lowest earners (45.2%). If we include those expressing more cautious support for this policy, the proportion rises to two-thirds of the respondents. This distribution reflects the general internalization of egalitarian ideology in the economic domain. However, this widespread economic radicalism appears inconsistent with the pattern of income differentiation that serves as a central mechanism in the economic reform program presently being pursued in Poland.

Conclusion

The data on objective differentiation presented in this paper do not correspond closely to images propagated by the Polish mass media. In particular, disparities in the average wages of occupational groups were actually smaller in 1980 than in 1976, a finding that runs counter to the generally held view. Our data do not lend support to the hypothesis that an increase in economic inequality accompanied the political crisis of the early 1980s. Perhaps such an increase occurred subsequently, as a side effect of the crisis; substantiation of this proposition would require further research.

On the other hand, our analysis of the state of social consciousness confirms the commonplace perception about the growth of social tension and discontent. Thus, the proportion of people citing significant social divisions and the conflict-engendering role of income, power, and nature of work increased during 1976–80. Identification of power as a factor producing conflict became more widespread. Our analysis indicated, however, that crystallization of views involving social conflict is not correlated with occupational categories. Similarly, party membership, trade-union affiliation, and education did not appear to be indicative of these views. Perhaps views shared by people across social-stratification divisions provided the basis for a new social integration, a necessary condition for the emergence of a social movement opposed to the political practices of the period 1976–80.

Notes

1. The basic variables of occupation, education, and other demographic characteristics were conceptualized and operationalized according to principles established by Daniłowicz et al. 1980; Wesołowski 1974; Pohoski and Słomczyński 1978; Słomczyński and Kacprowicz 1979.

2. See Malanowski 1967; Widerszpil and Janicki 1959; Nowak 1966; Tobera 1972.

3. Respondents who answered that a given factor currently generates conflict were asked whether the amount of conflict engendered was more, about the same, or less ten years ago; persons who asserted that a given factor does not produce conflict were asked whether in their opinion the same was true ten years ago.

References

Daniłowicz, P., J. Lutyński, A. Sianko, and P. B. Sztabiński
 1980 *Podstawowe kategorie klasyfikacyjne w zakresie zmiennych metryczkowych.* [Basic Classification Categories for Background Variables.] Warsaw: Institute of Philosophy and Sociology of the Polish Academy of Sciences.

Janicka, K.
 1976 *Ruchliwość międzypokoleniowa i jej korelaty.* [Intergenerational Mobility and Its Correlates.] Wrocław: Ossolineum.

Kobus-Wojciechowska, A.
 1977 *Położenie materialne i uczestnictwo w kulturze a struktura społeczna.* [Standard of Living, Participation in Culture and Social Structure.] Wrocław: Ossolineum.

Malanowski, J.
 1967 *Stosunki klasowe i różnice społeczne w mieście.* [Class Relations and Social Differentiation in an Urban Setting.] Warsaw: Polish Scientific Publishers.

Nowak, S.
 1966 "Psychologiczne aspekty przemian struktury społecznej i ruchliwości społecznej." [Psychological aspects of transformations of social structure and social mobility.] *Studia Socjologiczne*, No. 2(21):3–40.

Ossowski, S.
 1963 *Class Structure in the Social Consciousness.* London: Routledge and Kegan Paul.

Pohoski, M. and K.M. Słomczyński
 1978 *Społeczna klasyfikacja zawodów.* [Social Classification of Occupations.] Warsaw: Institute of Philosophy and Sociology of the Polish Academy of Sciences

Słomczyński, K.
 1972 *Zróżnicowanie społeczno-zawodowe i jego korelaty.* [Socio-occupational Differentiation and Its Correlates.] Wrocław: Ossolineum

Słomczyński, K. M. and G. Kacprowicz
 1979 *Skale zawodów.* [Scales of Occupations.] Warsaw: Institute of Philosophy and Sociology of the Polish Academy of Sciences.

Słomczyński, K. M. and W. Wesołowski
   1973   "Potoczne percepcje struktury społecznej." [Everyday perceptions of social structure.] Pp. 241–69 in K. Słomczyński and W. Wesołowski (eds.), *Struktura i ruchliwość społeczna*. [Social Structure and Mobility.] Wrocław: Ossolineum.
   1977   "Przemiany struktury społecznej i jej percepcji." [Transformations of social structure and its perceptions.] Paper presented at the Congress of the Polish Sociological Association. Cracow.

Słomczyński, K. M. and W. Wesołowski (eds.)
   1973   *Struktura i ruchliwość społeczna*. [Social Structure and Mobility.] Wrocław: Ossolineum.

Tobera, P.
   1972   *Zróżnicowanie społeczne pracowników przemysłu*. [Social Differentiation of Industrial Employees.] Warsaw: Polish Scientific Publishers.

Warzywoda-Kruszyńska, W.
   1974   *Małżeństwa a struktura społeczna*. [Marriage and Social Structure.] Wrocław: Ossolineum.

Wesołowski, W. (ed.)
   1970   *Zróżnicowanie społeczne*. [Social Differentiation.] Wrocław: Ossolineum.
   1974   *Standaryzacja zmiennych socjologicznych*. [Standardization of Sociological Variables.] Warsaw: Institute of Philosophy and Sociology of the Polish Academy of Sciences.

Widerszpil, S. and J. Janicki
   1959   "Do jakiej klasy należysz?" [To which class do you belong?] *Życie Gospodarcze*, No. 25 and 27.

The Attainment of Occupational Status
A Model with Multiple Indicator Constructs

KAZIMIERZ M. SŁOMCZYŃSKI

Introduction

In this paper we consider the model of status attainment formulated by Blau and Duncan (1967) and subsequently modified and extended (Duncan, Featherman, Duncan, 1972; Sewell and Hauser, 1975; Featherman and Hauser, 1976; Sewell, Hauser, and Featherman, 1976). In the original version of the model, the occupational status of an individual at a given time was represented as a linear function of that individual's occupational status at the beginning of his work career, that individual's education, and two variables characterizing the "inheritance" of social position: father's occupational status and father's education. We applied this model to Polish data, incorporating nonobservable variables inferred from multiple indicators. We estimated all coefficients of the model on the basis of variance-covariance matrices of observed variables, according to the maximum likelihood method. Two computer programs, LISREL (Jöreskog and Sörbom, 1978) and MILS (Schoenberg, 1981), were used.

Parts of this paper are taken from Słomczyński (1983). The author is indebted to Krystyna Janicka and Jadwiga Koralewicz-Zębik for their participation in the planning and administration of the study; to Bruce Roberts for computer assistance; and to Włodzimierz Wesołowski and Bogdan W. Mach for critical readings of earlier versions of the manuscript. The survey was conducted under the auspices and with the financial support of the Institute of Philosophy and Sociology of the Polish Academy of Sciences.

In a provocative paper Campbell (1983:59) notes: "We must realize that status attainment models provide a sophisticated numerical answer to questions about the balance between ascription and achievement at a particular point in time in a society with a particular structure and culture. Perhaps the most theoretically interesting questions one can ask involve the conditions under which the balance will change." We show that in Polish society at the end of the 1970s ascription variables (father's education and status) affected achievement variables (son's education and status) primarily at the beginning of the son's occupational career. A relatively weak correlation between father's status and son's status—weaker than has been found for Western European countries and the United States—indicates that in Poland the balance between ascription and achievement has already been changed. We provide new empirical evidence allowing for theorizing about the conditions under which this change occurs.

One of the recent refinements introduced into status attainment models is the use of multiple indicators to increase the reliability of measurement (e.g. Alwin and Jackson, 1980; Featherman et al., 1975; Hauser et al., 1983). Kerckhoff (1984) considers this refinement in the context of cross-national comparative studies. He points out that "comparative research would use indigenous [occupational] scales." Referring to education, he writes: "With the LISREL approach to multivariate analysis, it is possible to use multiple indices of a single concept and to derive a single effect estimate for the combination. It is thus possible to define educational attainment in ways that are consistent with each society's definition and still produce results that are compatible across societies" (150). In this paper we use various indigenous (Polish) occupational scales and various indicators of educational attainment appropriate for Poland.

Data

Empirical data are taken from a study on the psychological consequences of the work situation (Janicka et al., 1977), which is a partial replication of Kohn and Schooler (1978; Kohn, 1969; see also: Kohn and Schooler, 1983; Słomczyński et al., 1981). The Polish study was based on a representative sample of men, aged 19 to 65, living in urban areas. Interviews were carried out with 1,557 individuals, forming a sample with a high response rate. The questionnaire contained a number of items pertaining to the occupational career of a respondent, his education, and the social position of his family. Only the data on occupational attainment are utilized in the paper; for presentations and analyses of other data collected in this study, see Słomczyński et al., 1981; Miller et al., 1985; Kohn et al., 1986.

Measurement of occupational status

The detailed classifications of occupations range from a dozen or so to several hundred categories; these classifications serve as the basis for scales characterizing jobs in specific terms. Relevant examples include prestige scales (e.g. Rauhala, 1966; Siegel, 1971; Goldthorpe and Hope, 1974; Treiman, 1977; Jackson, 1976) and socioeconomic status scales (e.g. Duncan, 1961; Nam and Powers, 1968; Ellery and Irving, 1972; Blishen and McRoberts, 1976). Recently sociologists have also focused on scales describing other aspects of occupational differentiation such as job requisites (e.g. Temme, 1975) or complexity of work (e.g. Speath, 1979; Kohn, 1969; Kohn and Schooler, 1983). Still, two theoretical questions remain open to debate: which "dimensions" of occupational status should be distinguished, and at which level of the division and organization of labor should they be examined?

In this paper we consider three occupational scales: (1) skill requirements, (2) complexity of work, and (3) socioeconomic rewards. All three scales are defined for the narrow occupational categories contained in *Social Classification of Occupations* (Pohoski and Słomczyński, 1978); a full description of these scales can be found in Słomczyński and Kacprowicz (1979) and in Słomczyński (1980).

A. The scale of skill requirements

To construct a scale of skill requirements we utilized scores of "general educational development" (GED) and "specific vocational preparation" (SVP), originally provided in the *Dictionary of Occupational Titles* (U.S. Department of Labor, 1965). These scores were assigned to the categories of the Polish Social Classification of Occupations, using information from the U.S. census classification (Temme, 1975). In addition, we took a variable describing the educational level required for a given occupation from the 1973 Polish labor force data (Graczyk, 1975). In these data 122 occupations were classified as requiring college or university education, 63 as requiring secondary education, and 168 as requiring vocational education. We applied this distribution to the Social Classification of Occupations.

Correlation among the three variables turned out to be high ($r \geq .61$); obtained correlation coefficients were used in a confirmatory factor analysis to compute weights for constructing the synthetic variable—the skill-requirement scale. Generally, this scale differentiates occupations with respect to cognitive abilities and achievements needed for the satisfactory performance of jobs in these occupations.

B. The scale of the complexity of work

To establish the degree of complexity of work that involves people, symbols, or things, two major sources providing descriptions of work activity typical for given occupations were employed: *Systematyczny słownik zawodów* (Systematic Dictionary of Occupations) by the Central Statistical Office (1970), and *Encyklopedyczny przewodnik: zawody i specjalności w szkolnictwie zawodowym* (Encyclopedic Guide to Occupations and Specializations in Vocational Schools) by Polish Scientific Publishers (1973). Final coding was based on the results obtained from three sources: (1) original coding of all categories of the Social Classification of Occupations, undertaken by specialists;

(2) transferring symbols of an analogous code from categories in the *Dictionary of Occupational Titles* (U.S. Department of Labor, 1965); and (3) the expertise of work-study specialists who conducted analyses for certain categories.

Scores describing the complexity of work with people, symbols, and things were used to obtain a regression equation in which the dependent variable was the arithmetic mean of the substantive complexity of work, as defined in Kohn and Schooler (1983), and computed on the individual level (Janicka et al., 1983). Using this equation the scores of substantive complexity of work were estimated for all occupations. The scale shows the degree to which work in a given occupation requires thought and independent judgment.

C. *The scale of socioeconomic rewards*

In constructing a scale of socioeconomic rewards we utilized data collected in studies in Koszalin, Szczecin, and Łódź during the period 1964–67 (Wesołowski, 1970; Słomczyński, 1972; Słomczyński and Wesołowski, 1973; Kobus-Wojciechowska, 1977) and repeated on a smaller scale in 1976 (Wesołowski and Słomczyński, 1977). For 34 narrow occupational categories seven variables were determined: (1) monthly wages; (2) the prestige score; (3) the index of housing standards; (4) the index of ownership of durable goods; (5) the score of occupational position in the organization of work; (6) the score of cultural consumption; and (7) the number of years of schooling.[1] The value of each of these variables was an arithmetic mean of the values found in the given population. A description of variables 1, 2, 5, and 7 is provided in Słomczyński, 1972 (54–71, 85–93, 100–20; and of variables 3, 4, and 6, in Kobus-Wojciechowska, 1977 (78–87, 97–101, 206–9). These variables served to carry out an exploratory factor analysis. In effect, for each of the 34 occupational categories a value of the socioeconomic rewards index was calculated as a sum of the values of the standardized variables multiplied by their factor weights.

The calculated index was then regressed on the average educational level and average earnings of the matching occupational categories from the 1973 labor force census. Using the resulting equation, the values of the index for all occupational categories were computed. Słomczyński and Kacprowicz (1979) demonstrated the validity of the scale for the 1960s and 1970s. They also showed that the index could be interpreted in the same way as Duncan's (1961) SEI.

Multiple indicator measurement of educational level

In Poland significant progress has been recorded in recent years in the use of survey research to obtain information about the basic characteristics of a respondent's social position. This occurred largely because of the effort made to standardize questions pertaining to personal background (Wesołowski, 1974; Lutyński, 1977). In a monograph written by Daniłowicz and Sztabiński (1977) a proposal was put forward to define the content and form of questions that would deal with a respondent's educational level. The recommended battery of questions was adopted in a national study of the psychological consequences of the work situation (Janicka et al., 1977). One possible way of analyzing data collected with this method is discussed here.

We constructed four variables that measure the current educational level of the respondent; these include: (1) number of years of schooling; (2) type of education completed; (3) cost of education; and (4) the age at which formal education ended. The number of years of schooling is supplemented by the type of education completed to account for credentials recognized on the job market. The cost of education defines an indicator adopted mainly in the economics of education (Kluczyński, 1968; Andrzejak, 1979; Charkiewicz et al., 1968). The age at which a respondent completed his formal education has also been used in some studies (e.g. Treiman and Terrell, 1975).

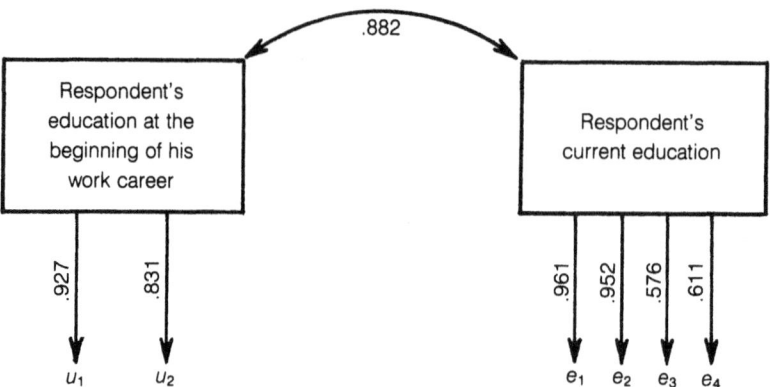

Figure 1. Measurement model for educational attainment in two time points. National sample, 1978.

All coefficients statistically significant ($p < .05$).
u_1, e_1—years of schooling.
u_2, e_2—type of education.
e_3—cost of education.
e_4—age at which education was completed.

These four variables were subjected to the factor-analytic measurement model of the respondent's educational attainment, as presented in Figure 1. The model includes educational attainment at the beginning of the respondent's work career, measured by only two indicators: number of years of schooling and type of schooling completed. The model fits the data well, with the ratio of chi-square to the degrees of freedom equal to 4.6.

The number of years of schooling and the type of education completed are very strong indicators of the current level of education. However, the path coefficients from the construct of educational attainment to two other indicators—the cost of education and the age at which formal education was completed—are also statistically significant, suggesting that these variables jointly measure the common latent variable.[2]

The indicators that have the highest values of the path coefficients for current educational level are included in the measurement of the respondent's educational level at the beginning of his work career. Since the path coefficients are large for two time

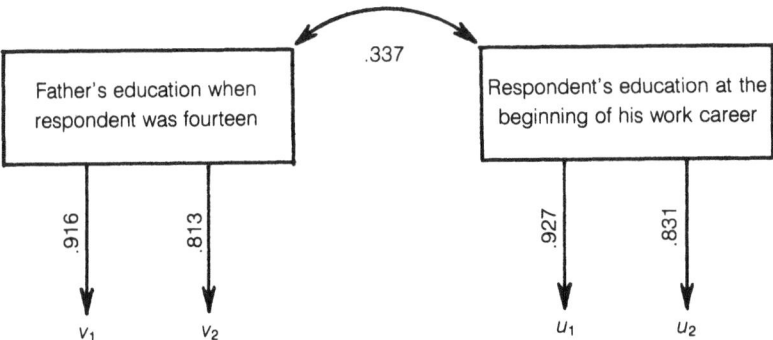

Figure 2. Measurement model for father's education and respondent's education. National sample, 1978.

All coefficients statistically significant ($p < .05$).

v_1, u_1—years of schooling.
v_2, u_2—type of education.

points ($p \geq .831$), the correlation between overall constructs for these points should be considered reliable. The level of education at the beginning of the work career explains about seventy-five percent of the variance of present educational attainment. This approximates the findings presented in Pohoski's (1979) study.

In this paper we examined the impact of both the father's educational attainment and the respondent's educational attainment at the beginning of his work career on the respondent's occupational status. For each person's educational attainment we used the two most reliable indicators, i.e., years of schooling and type of education. Figure 2 shows that path coefficients for these indicators are very high and similar for both generations—that of fathers and that of sons. Using this measurement, the correlation between educational levels of fathers and sons is .337.

The basic model of status attainment

Let us denote the father's educational level by V; the father's occupation at the time the respondent was fourteen by T; the respondent's educational level at the beginning of his work career by U; the respondent's first occupation by W; and the respon-

Table 1

Means, Standard Deviations, and Correlations of Scales for Father's Occupation and Respondent's First and Current Occupation. National Sample, 1978

Variables and occupational scales	Mean	Standard deviation	Correlation	
			Respondent's first occupation (W)	Respondent's current occupation (Y)
A. Skill requirements				
Father's occupation (T)	39.3	18.4	.259	.213
Respondent's first occupation (W)	32.5	19.8	1.000	.543
Respondent's current occupation (Y)	43.7	22.3	.543	1.000
B. Complexity of work				
Father's occupation (T)	41.9	14.0	.274	.235
Respondent's first occupation (W)	40.9	15.8	1.000	.545
Respondent's current occupation (Y)	48.4	15.9	.545	1.000
C. Socioeconomic rewards				
Father's occupation (T)	21.0	17.1	.320	.272
Respondent's first occupation (W)	23.2	17.2	1.000	.592
Respondent's current occupation (Y)	30.4	20.1	.592	1.000

dent's present occupation by Y. The educational levels of the father and the respondent (V, U) are expressed by two indicators: years of schooling (v_1, u_1) and type of schooling (v_2, u_2). The variables of occupational status (T, W, V) are expressed on three scales: skill requirements (t_1, w_1, y_1) complexity of work (t_2, w_2, y_2), and socioeconomic rewards (t_3, w_3, y_3).

Table 1 presents the means, standard deviations, and correlations for father's and son's occupational status. On each of the three scales—skill requirements, complexity of work, and socioeconomic rewards—the current status of the respondent (Y) is much higher than his status at the beginning of his career (W) or that of his father (T). Since the respondent's initial status (W) and the father's status (T) have similar mean values, "intergenerational advancement" (i.e., the difference between Y and T) is an effect of intragenerational increase in status.

A comparison of the distribution characteristics of variables Y and T, shows that an increase in variance of both these variables accompanies "intragenerational advancement." If the variance is treated as a measure of distributive inequality (Jencks, 1972; Allison, 1978), we can claim that intergenerational advancement has occurred in the situation of increasing status inequality which was brought about by economic development.

The father's occupation (T) is more strongly correlated with the respondent's first occupation (W) than it is with the respondent's present occupation (Y). However, the difference between correlations is not large: $.039 \leq r_{tw} - r_{ty} \leq .048$, when $.249 \leq r_{tw} \leq .320$ and $.213 \leq r_{ty} \leq .272$. The correlation which expresses intragenerational stability is significantly higher: $.543 \leq r_{wy} \leq .592$. In general, such a relation among correlations is consistent with the results of research obtained in various countries, including socialist ones (Safar, 1971).

The correlation between the father's occupation (T) and the respondent's present occupation (Y) represents the most general measure of the rigidity of the stratification system. This correlation, which varies from .213 to .272, does not substantially differ from the ones we additionally computed for various national samples. In our computations we utilized data from Nowak's (1966) study, conducted in 1962 on a sample of adult urban males; from Sarapata's (1965) study, conducted in 1962 on a representative sample of adult urban and rural residents; and from Zagórski's (1976) study, conducted in 1972 on a sample of working men and women. In addition, we utilized unpublished data from a study conducted in 1975 on a representative sample of men.[3] For all these studies correlations between the father's occupation (T) and the respondent's present occupation (Y) range

Table 2

Correlations between Scales for Father's Occupation and Respondent's First and Current Occupation. National Sample, 1978

Pairs of occupational scales	Father's occupation (T)	Respondent's first occupation (W)	Respondent's current occupation (Y)
Skill requirements and complexity of work	.878	.903	.896
Skill requirements and socioeconomic rewards	.703	.882	.863
Complexity of work and socioeconomic rewards	.842	.903	.901

from .209 to .313. The correlations found in our study are well within this range.

The value of father–son correlation depends on the occupational scale. This is a consequence of the fact that the scales are not identical; they measure distinctive aspects of occupational status. Table 2 shows that the correlations between occupational scales range from .703 to .903. Generally, for the father's status (T) and for the respondent's statuses (W, Y), the skill requirements scale is less strongly correlated with the socioeconomic rewards scale than is either of these two scales with that of the complexity of work.

Table 3 shows that the correlations between each of the two indicators of educational attainment with occupational scales differ. If we consider that each educational measurement can be related to each occupational scale, the difference in estimates of correlations may lead to contradictory conclusions. To substantiate this it is sufficient to compare the correlation of the father's educational level (V) and his occupational status (T) for two pairs of measurement: (1) years of schooling and skill requirements (for which the correlation is moderate, i.e., .463), and (2) type of education and socioeconomic rewards (for which the correlation is strong, i.e., .689). Also, the differences in correlations of the father's occupational status (T) and the respondent's education

Table 3

Correlation among Educational and Occupational Variables of Respondent's Father and Respondent. National Sample, 1978

Educational variables	Occupational variables		
	Father's occupation (T)	Respondent's first occupation (W)	Respondent's current occupation (Y)
Education of the respondent's father (V)			
Skill requirements			
1. Years of schooling	.463	.300	.238
2. Type of school	.465	.271	.219
Complexity of work			
1. Years of schooling	.583	.311	.266
2. Type of school	.580	.274	.244
Socioeconomic rewards			
1. Years of schooling	.688	.310	.281
2. Type of school	.689	.279	.258
Education of respondent (U)			
Skill requirements			
1. Years of schooling	.215	.572	.484
2. Type of school	.212	.575	.477
Complexity of work			
1. Years of schooling	.268	.590	.520
2. Type of school	.259	.570	.507
Socioeconomic rewards			
1. Years of schooling	.321	.596	.545
2. Type of school	.302	.624	.553

(U) appear substantial since in some cases they exceed .100.

It seemed justifiable to incorporate the various indicators of education and the various indicators of status into one common model which would relate the measurement part with the causal part. We included all four variables (v_1, v_2; u_1, u_2) describing education (V, U), and nine variables (t_1, t_2, t_3; w_1, w_2, w_3; y_1, y_2, y_3) describing status (T, W, Y) into the LISREL/MILS program. Since education variables led to linear dependency, we fixed the appropriate measurement coefficients at values given in Figure 2.

Figure 3 presents the final version of our model and it includes both the measurement and causal parts. The measurement part of the model confirms that all three occupational scales are good indicators of status for both the respondent and his father. In all instances, the socioeconomic rewards scale is the weakest indicator of occupational status. Allowing for some correlations among residuals of the scales modifies path coefficients to only a small extent; because of that, we fixed all correlations of residuals to zero.

In our model we hypothesize that the education of the respondent (U) affects his first (W) and current (Y) status; status W influences status Y. We also assume that father's education (V) affects respondent's education (U) and that father's status (T) influences both statuses of the son (W, Y). These assumptions are consistent with the basic model of status attainment developed by Blau and Duncan (1967). The absence of causal influences of father's education (V) on either occupational status of the son (W, Y) will be discussed later. The consequences of weakening these assumptions will also be examined.

The model fits data well; the chi-square statistic is 4.1 per one degree of freedom. Considering the estimates of our model, we should take into account the implied correlations between all constructs (Table 4). According to our model the correlation between father's (T) and son's current (Y) status is low (.229); the variable T explains only a little over 5 percent of variance in Y. As can be seen from Figure 3, the direct effect of T on Y becomes reduced significantly to .075, by about 33 percent. Since

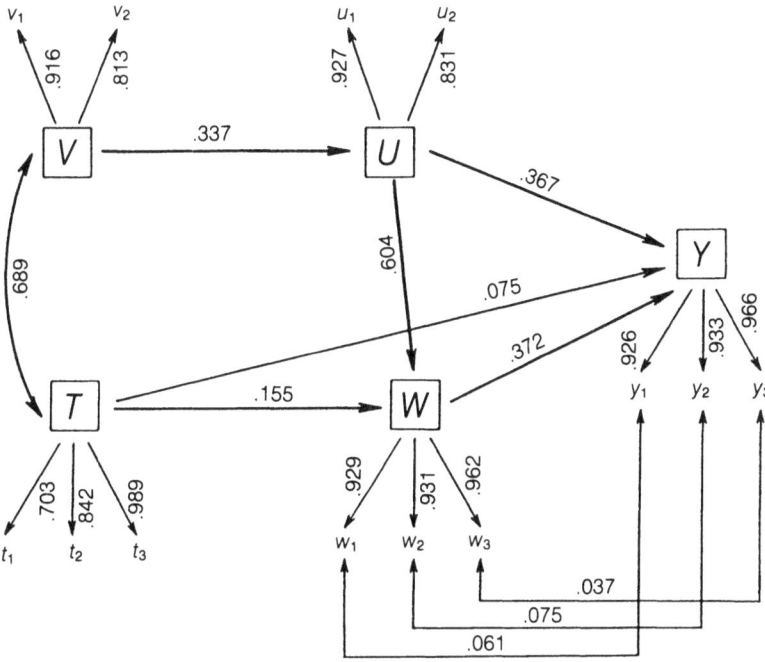

Figure 3. Basic model of status attainment for Polish men, aged 19 to 65, living in urban areas in 1978.

V—father's education.
S—father's occupation.
U—respondent's education at the beginning of the work career.
W—respondent's first occupation.
Y—respondent's current occupation.

v_1, u_1—years of schooling.
v_2, u_2—type of education.
t_1, w_1, y_1—scale of skill requirements.
t_2, w_2, y_2—scale of complexity of work.
t_3, w_3, y_3—scale of socioeconomic rewards.

Measurement coefficients for V and U are fixed at values from Figure 2. All other coefficients statistically significant ($p < .05$).

Table 4

Correlations among Constructs of Basic Model of Status Attainment. National Sample, 1978

		V	T	U	W	Y
Father's education	(V)	1.000	.689	.337	.310	.263
Father's occupation	(T)		1.000	.232	.295	.229
Respondent's education	(U)			1.000	.640	.613
Respondent's first occupation	(W)				1.000	.617
Respondent's current occupation	(Y)					1.000

the indirect effect represents about 45 percent of the entire correlation, 22 percent is attributable to a spurious relationship.

This does not mean, however, that the occupational career of an individual is not determined by variables relating to social origin. Let us note that not only does the father's education (V) significantly influence the respondent's education (U), but also the father's occupational status (T) affects the respondent's starting position (W). These two effects (.337 and .155) indicate that life chances at the outset of a career are clearly dependent on ascribed factors.

If we weaken our assumption and allow for the direct impact of the father's education on the respondent's present occupational status, this impact is found statistically insignificant and the fit of the model is worse. When the value of the coefficient r for the influence of father's occupation on respondent's present occupation is relatively low, the proposition that ascribed values decrease in influence during a career is lent further weight.

For the entire correlation between the respondent's education and his first occupational status ($r_{uw} = .640$), the causal effect is clearly dominant ($\beta = .604$) and constitutes over 90 percent. Starting with the beginning of a career, both these variables have a similar influence on its subsequent development. The entire correlations between education and occupational status from the period of the first job to present status are similar (.613 ≤ .617) and they are more or less characterized to the same degree by direct causal relationships ($\beta_{yu} = .367$ and $\beta_{yw} = .372$). Generally, therefore, not only are the influences of social origin on present occupational status weak, they are further reduced by the impact of the beginning of the work career.

Extended model of status attainment

Critics of the basic model of occupational status attainment may argue that certain important variables are overlooked. In particular, it became obvious that education at the beginning of the work career should be supplemented by current education. In Poland the measurement of educational attainment at two time points seems justified given the significant proportion of the population who increase their education during their occupational career (Zagórski, 1976). In the remaining part of our analysis we shall express the respondent's current education, denoted by E, as a synthetic index constructed on the basis of the four weighted indicators included in the measurement model presented in Figure 1. Among the variables characterizing some ascribed factors, we looked at the urbanness of the place (denoted by R) where the respondent was brought up until age fourteen. For control purposes we also included the respondent's age (A).

In the model presented in Figure 4 we hypothesize that all residual values of variables are not correlated with each other. The model fits the data well, with the ratio of chi-square to the degrees of freedom being 5.6. Table 5 complements Figure 4 and gives correlations for the new variables.

The influence of initial education (U) is strong in relation to both the occupational status at the time of the first job (W) and later education (E). In turn, later education (E) affects current occupational status (Y) to almost the same degree as "starting" education (U) affects occupational status at the first job (W). These are the strongest relationships in the model; the respective coefficients range from .613 to .691.

Occupational status at the first job (W) affects current status (Y)

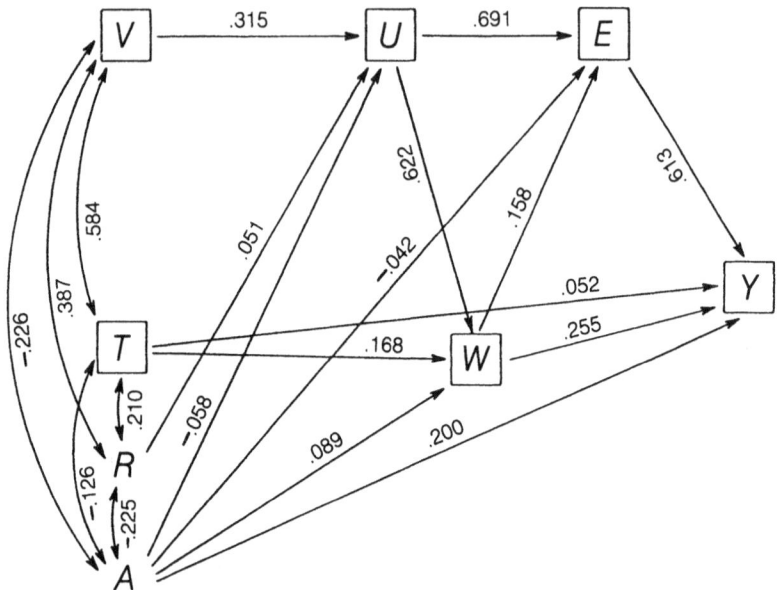

Figure 4. Extended model of status attainment for Polish men, aged 19 to 65, living in urban areas in 1978.

All coefficients statistically significant ($p < .05$).

V—father's education.
T—father's occupation.
U—respondent's education at the beginning of the work career.
W—respondent's first occupation.
Y—respondent's current occupation.
E—respondent's current education.
R—the size of locality in which the respondent resided when he was fourteen.
A—respondent's age.

The unobserved variables (V, T, U, W, Y, E) are inferred from several indicators with measurement coefficients estimated in this model (T, W, Y) or in separate measurement models (V, U, E) given in Figures 1 and 2. Variables R and A are observable directly.

Table 5

Correlations of Constructs of the Basic model of Status Attainment with Current Education, Urbanness, and Age. National Sample, 1978.

Constructs of basic model		Respondent's current education[a] (E)	Urbanness[b] (R)	Respondent's age (A)
Father's education	(V)	.288	.387	−.226
Father's occupation	(T)	.185	.210	−.126
Respondent's education	(U)	.882	.160	−.135
Respondent's first occupation	(W)	.603	.109	−.015
Respondent's current occupation	(Y)	.740	.068	.111

[a] For measurement of current education see Figure 1.
[b] Measured by size of community in which respondent resided when he was fourteen.

more strongly than present education (E). These effects show the relatively minor role played by starting status on the course of the subsequent educational and work career. In comparison with the basic model (Figure 3), we notice a marked reduction of occupational stability. This is a result of introducing a measurement of educational attainment at the second time-point into the model.

The father's education (V) has a greater impact than his occupational status (T) on the entire process described by the model. This increased significance is based on the determination of the "starting" education of the son, expressed by $\beta_{uv} = .315$. It should be emphasized that both coefficients of "inheritance" of the occupational status, β_{wt} and β_{yt}, are low. In particular, the net effect of the father's occupational status (T) on the respondent's current occupational status (Y), is .052—low, but still significant $(p \leq .05)$.

The degree of urbanness of the place in which the respondent was brought up (R) affects education only before the first job (U). The impact of age (A) goes in two directions: the older the individual, the relatively lower his education (U, E) and the relatively higher his occupational status (W, Y). The effect of age on present occupational status (.200) is substantial; it is stronger than the effect of the father's status (T) on the son's status (Y).

The relationships described remain stable if other variables are introduced into the analysis. In further efforts to modify the model, we took into account the number of children the respondent had, the educational level of his wife, and membership in voluntary organizations. When these variables were incorporated into the model in a proper cause–effect structure, their direct impact on occupational status was shown to be statistically insignificant.

Conclusion

Our analysis has been directed toward an explication of educational and occupational attainment, using the multiple indicator conceptualization of both types of attainment. Years of schooling and type of education were used to measure the educational attainment of fathers and respondents at the beginning of their work careers. Occupational status was defined by three scales: skill requirements, complexity of work, and socioeconomic rewards. The basic model of status attainment including these indicators shows complex relationships between ascribed and achieved factors.

For Polish men aged 19 to 65, living in cities, the correlation between their occupational status and that of their fathers varies from .213 to .272, depending on occupational scales. When three scales—skill requirements, complexity of work, and socioeconomic rewards—are employed in the multiple indicator model of status attainment, the implied father–son correlation is .229. This is a lower correlation than is usually found in Western Europe (Svalastoga and Rishøj, 1965) or the United States.

Since the father's occupation affects the son's starting occupational status, and sons do eventually change their jobs, the net intergenerational effect on the son's current status is small. In the basic model, in which we take into account the father's and son's education along with the son's starting status, this effect is only

.075. It decreases even further when we introduce additional variables, such as the respondent's age or the degree of urbanness of the place where he was raised.

In Poland the ascribed variables (father's education and status) have a relatively small influence on the current status of the son. The principal factor explaining the current occupational status of men is their educational attainment. Simultaneously, ascribed variables affect men's achievement at the beginning of their work careers. The relatively strong impact of the father's education and status on the son's education and first job is caused by close family ties during early adulthood. In particular, a large proportion of young adults in Poland live with their parents not only during their entire educational career but also when they start their first job and even for some years after they marry.

In the model of status attainment presented in this paper psychological variables were not considered. Some researchers have been concerned with these variables, in particular with the role of intelligence (IQ) as a variable intervening in the relationship between father's and son's statuses (e.g. Jencks, 1972; Psacharopoulos, 1977). We did not include an IQ measurement in our study, but we did obtain a variable that can be incorporated into the model in place of IQ. This variable is intellectual (ideational) flexibility (IF), the construct introduced by Kohn and Schooler (1978); the measurement model of IF for Polish data is presented in Miller et al. (1985).

In Poland the correlation between intellectual flexibility and current occupational status is .503. This is a result consistent with the value of the correlation between occupational status and IQ found in a number of studies in many countries (for a review see Klarkowski, 1981: 103–5). The correlation between IF and education (.742) is somewhat higher than the average correlation between IQ and education (.650) for thirteen studies conducted in Western Europe and the United States (Klarkowski, 1981: 105).

In a complementary study (Słomczyński, 1983) the net effect of intellectual flexibility on occupational status was analyzed (that is, after controlling for other variables). This effect is statistically significant ($p \leq .05$). However, if intellectual flexibility is taken into account, the effect of the father's occupational status on that of the son disappears completely. In the United States and Great Britain it was found that the effect of father's status remained statistically significant in models of status attainment that included IQ (Psacharopoulos, 1977). Therefore, the general proposition that in Poland the net effect of the father's status on the son's is lower than in advanced capitalist countries seems to be valid. However, two qualifications should be made.

First, the process of attaining occupational status in Poland displays a specific structure: the father's occupational status rather strongly determines both the son's education and his first occupational status. Since education and initial occupational status play a key role in a person's subsequent occupational career, the effect of the father's status is eliminated by these variables. The fact that "inheritance" takes place at the outset of the process of status attainment does not reduce its importance.

Second, after World War II major transformations in occupational structure occurred in Poland. It remains to be determined whether the degree to which occupational status is inherited is smaller in Poland, in comparison with other countries, simply because of forced structural changes. We cannot preclude the possibility that the net effect of the father's status on that of the son would be much higher, if persons affected by structural mobility were excluded from comparative studies.

Taking into account the various limitations of our sample and survey design, we need to be cautious in interpreting the results of this study in cross-national perspective. However, two results differentiating Poland from Western Europe and the United States are rather well established: first, in Poland the correlation between father's status and son's status is weaker; and, second, in Poland the impact of educational attainment on status attainment is stronger (Słomczyński, 1983). These two results constitute empirical evidence of the change in balance between ascription and achievement, corresponding to the Polish government's goals of "less inheritance" and "more meritocracy." The analysis of conditions under which this change occurred remains to be undertaken.

Notes

1. Although the original socioeconomic scale includes education as one of its composite variables, it does not change substantially without this variable (Słomczyński and Kacprowicz, 1979: 92-3).
2. In our study the correlations among four indicators of educational attainment are stronger than the correlations among four different indicators of educational attainment analyzed by Kerckhoff et al. (1982) for Great Britain. In Poland, the cost of education and the age at which formal education ended may function as implicit credentialing criteria; both of these variables are indicators of the financial and psychological investment in the educational process.
3. A description of this sample is given in Alestalo et al. (1978).

References

Alestalo, M., K.M. Słomczyński, and W. Wesołowski
    1978   "Patterns of social stratification." Pp. 136-42 in E. Allardt and W. Wesołowski (eds.), *Social Structure and Change. Finland and Poland in Comparative Perspective*. Warsaw: Polish Scientific Publishers.

Allison, P.
    1978   "Measures of inequality." *American Sociological Review* 43:865-80.

Alwin, D.F. and D.J. Jackson
    1980   "Measurement models for response errors in surveys: issues and applications." In: K.F. Schuessler (ed.), *Sociological Methodology 1980*. San Francisco: Jossey-Bass.

Andrzejak, J.
    1979   *Koszty kształcenia w szkolnictwie ogólnokształcącym i zawodowym w latach 1966-1977*. [Cost of Education in General and Vocational Schools in the Years 1966-1977.] Warsaw: Central Statistical Office.

Blau, P. and O.D. Duncan
    1967   *The American Occupational Structure*. New York: Wiley.

Blishen, B.R. and H.A. McRoberts
    1976   "A revised socioeconomic index for occupations in Canada." *Canadian Review of Sociology and Anthropology* 13:71-9.

Campbell, R.T.
    1983   "Status attainment research: end of the beginning or beginning of the end?" *Sociology of Education* 56:47-62.

Central Statistical Office

1970 *Systematyczny słownik zawodów*. [Systematic Dictionary of Occupations.] Warsaw: Central Statistical Office.

Charkiewicz, M., J. Kluczyński, and A. Solarz
1968 "Wydatki z budżetu państwa na kształcenie w latach 1951-1955." [State budget expenditures for education in the years 1951-1955]. In: J. Kluczyński (ed.), *Ekonomiczno-społeczne aspekty kształcenia*. [Socioeconomic Aspects of Education.] Warsaw: Książka i Wiedza.

Daniłowicz, P. and P.B. Sztabiński
1977 Pytania metryczkowe. Wersja obowiązująca w Problemie 11.2 [Background Questions. Obligatory Version for Problem 11.2] Warsaw: The Institute of Philosophy and Sociology of the Polish Academy of Sciences. Mimeograph.

Duncan, O.D.
1961 "A socio-economic index for all occupations." Pp. 109-59 in A.J. Reiss, O.D. Duncan, P.K. Hatt, and C.C. North (eds.), *Occupational and Social Status*. New York: Free Press.

Duncan, O.D., D. Featherman, and B. Duncan
1972 *Socioeconomic Background and Achievement*. New York: Seminar Press.

Ellery, W. and J.C. Irving
1972 "Socioeconomic index for New Zealand based on levels of education and income from the 1966 census." *New Zealand Journal of Educational Studies* 7:153-67.

Featherman, D.L. and R.M. Hauser
1976 "Prestige or socioeconomic scales in the study of occupational achievement?" *Sociological Methods and Research* 4:403-22.

Featherman, D.L., F.L. Jones and R.M. Hauser
1975 "Assumptions of social mobility research in the U.S.: the case of occupational status." *Social Science Research* 4:329-60.

Goldthorpe, J.H., and K. Hope
1974 *The Social Grading of Occupations. A New Approach and Scale*. Oxford: Clarendon Press.

Graczyk, B.
1975 "Zawód wyuczony i wykonywany według danych spisu kadrowego 1973." [Occupation learned and performed in the data of occupational census 1973]. *Wiadomości Statystyczne* 9:23-31.

Hauser, R.M., S. Tsai and W.H. Sewell
1983 "A model of stratification with response error in social and psychological variables." *Sociology of Education* 56: 26-46.

Jackson, J.J.
1976 "The Irish occupational index: a new scale for coding Irish occupational data." Paper presented at the meeting of the Research Committee on Social Stratification of the International Sociological Association. Dublin, Ireland, April 5-7.

Janicka, K., G. Kacprowicz, and K. M. Słomczyński

1983 "Złożoność pracy jako zmienna socjologiczna." [Complexity of work as a sociological variable]. Studia Socjologitzne No. 3 (90): 5-33.
Janicka, K., J. Koralewicz-Zębik, and K.M. Słomczyński
1977 "Wymiary sytuacji pracy i ich psychospołeczne konsekwencje: projekt badawczy." [Dimensions of the work situation and their psycho-social consequences: a research project]. Warsaw: Institute of Philosophy and Sociology of the Polish Academy of Sciences.
Jencks, C.
1972 *Inequality. A Reassessment of the Effects of Family and Schooling in America.* New York: Basic Books.
Jöreskog, K.G. and D. Sörbom
1978 *LISREL IV—A General Computer Program for Estimation of a Linear Structural System by Maximum Likelihood Methods.* Chicago, Ill.: International Educational Service.
Kerckhoff, A.C.
1984 "The current state of social mobility research." *Sociological Quarterly* 25: 139-53.
Kerckhoff, A.C., R.T. Campbell and J.M. Trott
1982 "Dimensions of educational and occupational attainment in Great Britain." *American Sociological Review* 47: 347-64.
Klarkowski, A.
1981 "Rola zdolności intelektualnych w reprodukcji struktury społecznej" [The role of intellectual abilities in the reproduction of social structure] Pp. 99-120 in K.M. Słomczyński and W. Wesołowski (eds.), *Zróżnicowanie społeczne w perspektywie porównawczej.* [Social Differentiation in Comparative Perspective.] Wrocław: Ossolineum.
Kluczyński, J. (ed.)
1968 *Ekonomiczno-społeczne aspekty kształcenia.* [Socio-economic Aspects of Education.] Warsaw: Książka i Wiedza.
Kobus-Wojciechowska, A.
1977 *Położenie materialne i uczestnictwo w kulturze a struktura społeczna.* [Standard of Living, Participation in Culture, and Social Structure.] Wrocław: Ossolineum.
Kohn, M.L.
1969 *Class and Conformity. A Study in Values.* Homewood, Ill.: The Dorsey Press. (Second edition, 1977, published by the University of Chicago Press.)
Kohn, M.L. and C. Schooler
1978 "The reciprocal effects of the substantive complexity of work and intellectual flexibility: A longitudinal assessment." *American Journal of Sociology* 84:24-52.
Kohn, M.L. and C. Schooler (with the collaboration of J. Miller, K.A. Miller, C. Schoenbach, and R. Schoenberg)
1983 *Work and Personality: An Inquiry Into the Impact of Social Stratifi*

cation. Norwood, N.J.: Ablex.

Kohn, M.L., K. Słomczyński, and C. Schoenbach
1986 "Social stratification and the transmission of values in the family: a cross-national assessment." *Sociological Forum* I, No. 1.

Lutyński, J.
1977 "Uwagi wstępne" [Introductory remarks]. In: Pytania metryczkowe. Wersja obowiązująca w problemie 11.2 [Background Questions. Obligatory Version for Problem 11.2.] Warsaw: The Institute of Philosophy and Sociology of the Polish Academy of Sciences. Mimeograph.

Miller, J., K.M. Słomczyński, and M.L. Kohn
1985 "Continuity of learning-generalization: the effect of job on the intellective processes in the United States and Poland." *American Journal of Sociology* 91: 593–615.

Nam, C.B. and M.G. Powers
1968 "Changes in the relative status level of workers in the United States." *Social Forces* 43:158–77.

Nowak, S.
1966 "Psychologiczne aspekty przemian struktury społecznej i ruchliwości społecznej" [Psychological aspects of change in social structure and mobility]. *Studia Socjologiczne* No. 2 (21):75–107.

Pohoski, M.
1979 "Proces osiągnięć społeczno-zawodowych w Polsce" [The process of socio-occupational attainment in Poland]. In: Central Statistical Office (ed.), *Tendencje rozwoju społecznego* [Trends in the Social Development.] Warsaw: Central Statistical Office.

Pohoski, M. and K.M. Słomczyński
1978 *Społeczna klasyfikacja zawodów*. [Social Classification of Occupations.] Warsaw: Institute of Philosophy and Sociology of the Polish Academy of Sciences.

Polish Scientific Publishers
1973 *Encyklopedyczny przewodnik: zawody i specjalności w szkolnictwie zawodowym*. [Encyclopedic Guide to Occupations and Specializations in Vocational Schools.] Warsaw: Polish Scientific Publishers.

Psacharopoulos, G.
1977 "Family background, education, and achievement: A path model of earnings determinants in the U.K. and some alternatives." *British Journal of Sociology* 28:321–35.

Rauhala, U.
1966 *Suomalaisen yhteiskunnan sosiaalinen kerrostuneisuus*. [The Social Stratification of Finnish Society.] Pervoo: WSOY.

Safar, Z.
1971 "Basic data on social differentiation in Czechoslovak society." A corrected version of the paper presented at the Seventh World Congress of Sociology. Varna, Bulgaria. August 10–14.

Sarapata, A.
   1965   *Studia nad uwarstwieniem i ruchliwością społeczną w Polsce.* [Studies on Social Stratification and Mobility in Poland.] Warsaw: Książka i Wiedza.
Schoenberg, R.
   1981   *Documentation for MILS (Multiple Indicator for Linear Structural Models).* Bethesda, Md.: National Institute of Mental Health.
Sewell, W.H. and R.M. Hauser
   1975   *Education, Occupation, and Earnings.* New York: Seminar Press.
Sewell, W.H., R.M. Hauser, and D.L. Featherman (eds.)
   1976   *Schooling and Achievement in American Society.* New York: Seminar Press.
Siegel, P.M.
   1971   "Prestige in the American occupational structures." Chicago: University of Chicago. Mimeograph.
Słomczyński, K.M.
   1983   *Pozycja zawodowa i jej związki z wykształceniem.* [Occupational Status and Its Relation to Education.] Warsaw: The Institute of Philosophy and Sociology of the Polish Academy of Sciences.
   1980   "Skala zawodów według wymogów kwalifikacyjnych" [The scale of occupations according to skill requirements]. Warsaw: The Institute of Sociology of the University of Warsaw. Mimeograph.
   1972   *Zróżnicowanie społeczno-zawodowe i jego korelaty.* [Socio-occupational Differentiation and Its Correlates.] Wrocław: Ossolineum.
Słomczyński, K.M. and G. Kacprowicz
   1979   *Skale zawodów.* [Occupational Scales.] Warsaw: The Institute of Philosophy and Sociology of the Polish Academy of Sciences.
Słomczyński, K.M., J. Miller, and M.L. Kohn
   1981   "Stratification, work, and values: A Polish-United States comparison." *American Sociological Review* 46:720–44.
Słomczyński, K.M. and W. Wesołowski (eds.)
   1973   *Struktura i ruchliwość społeczna.* [Social Structure and Social Mobility.] Wrocław: Ossolineum.
Speath, J.L.
   1979   "Vertical differentiation among occupations." *American Sociological Review* 44:746–62.
Svalastoga, K. and T. Rishøj
   1965   "Social mobility: the Western European model." *Acta Sociologica* 9:175–82.
Temme, L.
   1975   *Occupations: Meaning and Measures.* Washington, D.C.: Bureau of Social Science Research.
Treiman, D.
   1977   *Occupational Prestige in Comparative Perspective.* New York: Academic Press.

Treiman, D. and K. Terrell
- 1975 "The process of status attainment in the United States and Great Britain." *American Sociological Review* 81:563-83.

U.S. Department of Labor
- 1965 *Dictionary of Occupational Titles.* Washington, D.C.: U.S. Government Printing Office.

Wesołowski, W. (ed.)
- 1970 *Zróżnicowanie społeczne.* [Social Differentiation.] (Second edition, 1974). Wroclaw: Ossolineum.
- 1974 *Standaryzacja zmiennych socjologicznych.* [Standardization of Sociological Variables.] Volume 1. Warsaw: The Institute of Philosophy and Sociology of the Polish Academy of Sciences.

Wesołowski, W. and K.M. Słomczyński
- 1977 "Przemiany struktury społecznej i jej percepcji" [Transformations of social structure and its perception]. Paper presented at the Fifth Congress of the Polish Sociological Association. Kraków, Poland. January 25-27.

Zagórski, K.
- 1976 *Zmiany struktury i ruchliwość społeczno-zawodowa w Polsce.* [Changes of Structure and Socio-occupational Mobility in Poland.] Warsaw: Central Statistical Office.

Dichotomous Class Images and Worker Radicalism

WOJCIECH ZABOROWSKI

Introduction

This paper explores the images of social structure among the working class and the intelligentsia. What will be analyzed is the psychological perception of society as being composed of two social classes, as well as the determinants and consequences of such a perception. Although the cognitive act of dividing social structure into a given number of social classes is but a superficial manifestation of class awareness or class consciousness, we take such an act seriously. Some sociologists have employed the variable "the number of social classes" to describe images of social structure (e.g. Tumin and Feldman, 1961; Cohen, 1968; Moorhouse, 1976). Doubts about the utility of this variable seem justified, if the goal of the research is to foster an understanding of the images of a social structure in all its subtle complexity (see Westergaard and Resler, 1975). Toward this end, the majority of techniques used to analyze survey data serve only to deform or oversimplify reality (Hiller, 1975: 6). However, straightforward information concerning the number of social classes is significant if treated as an explanatory variable. We present empirical support for the thesis that the two-class model (mental image) of

---

The research was conducted at the Institute of Sociology of the University of Warsaw and sponsored by the Institute of Philosophy and Sociology of the Polish Academy of Sciences. The initial description of the research project is given in Słomczyński, Soszyńska, and Zaborowski (1977).

society is, on the one hand, the effect of certain properties of an individual's social standing and, on the other, a condition that facilitates the formulation of radical social demands. The analysis is not confined to a particular type of two-class division such as, for example, the relations of asymmetric dependency (Ossowski, 1963: 31). In this study dichotomous images are considered to be any divisions of society into two parts. The variable constructed includes both analytical and normative definitions of social classes. Descriptive statements are characteristic of analytical definitions while evaluations based on superiority–inferiority or even moral judgments dominate normative responses. The descriptive and evaluative elements are usually closely interwoven.

Generally, three types of dichotomous images are distinguished: (1) those subsuming the entirety of the social structure—for example, the ruling class and the rest of society; (2) those focusing on the extremes found in the social hierarchy, leaving the middle ground undefined, as in the case of a division into rich and poor; and (3) those based on the juxtaposition of two groups whose characteristics are related to their functional role in society, such as office workers and manual workers. We aggregate the three types, since they display similar relationships to other variables. We label all of them "dichotomous images."

We will search for a determinant of the broad, internally differentiated categories of dichotomous images at each of two levels of analysis—individuals and groups. This strategy will allow us to "reconcile" explanations based on the distribution of individual attributes—in particular, level of education (Lewis, 1964; Lopreato and Hazelrigg, 1972)—and explanations focusing on the nature of primary-group interaction (Lockwood, 1966).

An individual's formulation of a particular classification of society may in turn promote certain attitudes. Our research enables us to establish a relationship between dichotomous images "rooted" in the social consciousness of workers and their radical demands for an egalitarian form of income distribution, participation in the management of economic enterprises, and in the exercise of political power. Although radical demands represent the program of a minority of the working class, the social importance of these demands results from such characteristics among its proponents as shared frustration, psychological support within the collectivity, and the role they play in the economic system.

Integration of the two levels of explanation, individual and group, is needed in order to fulfill an important objective of research on social stratification: to understand how individuals' frustrations are transformed into patterns of action characteristic of deprived groups. Focusing on this process allows us to understand better how a recruitment base for adherents of programs of social change is formed. This objective is consistent with the proposal advanced by Ossowski (1963: 6–7), that research on perceptions of social structure should be, in effect, research on the social functioning of ideology.

Method

Empirical data were gathered in 1979. Two sets of interviews, separated by a five-week interval, were conducted with a randomly selected sample of 330 men, aged 19 to 65, gainfully employed and living permanently in Warsaw. A questionnaire was used in which some of the items dealing with perceptions of social structure were repeated, allowing us to record a change in the opinions of the respondents. The repeated questions concerned the existence of social classes in Poland, and encouraged the respondents to identify the elements perceived in the social structure. The images of social structure found in respondents' answers were divided into dichotomous ones and those made up of more than two elements. A separate series of open-ended questions explored class self-identification and evaluations of the class affiliation of close friends.

During the preparation of the research design (Słomczyński, Soszyńska, and Zaborowski, 1977) we sought to establish a procedure that would stimulate respondents to give detailed information about social structure. We accordingly devised a questionnaire with a series of open-ended questions. Carefully selected, experienced, and well-trained interviewers carried out the fieldwork.

The end result provided rich empirical documentation that proved useful in a qualitative analysis. The material consists of the subjective "stories" of respondents about social structure and the social order. The technique of intersubjective interpretation enabled us to classify answers into various types; the radical type is the subject of this paper.[1]

Answers that were classified as indicating a radical type of perception of the social order were those that included emphasis on its unjust nature, a perception of conflict between opposed group interests, a perception of class domination, and arguments in favor of a change in the status quo. The radical type subsumed all respondents who expressed criticism of the perceived reality as well as those having a more general predisposition toward change. The "radicals" were differentiated by the preferred direction of the social change they desired. Information about this was derived from a series of questions concerning economic egalitarianism, the influence of workers in the management of enterprises, and the scope of society's control over the political authorities and vice versa.

The interview also furnished basic information about the social position of the respondents, their level of education, earnings, family income, housing conditions, and occupational status and status changes. In addition, information was collected about the extensiveness of the respondent's social contacts. He was asked about both formal and informal interactions at work, and about social relations.

Findings: social position and the dichotomous image of social structure

Manual workers perceive society in dichotomous terms more often than do members of other occupational groups. The workers' level of skills has only a small influence on the likelihood of their adopting a dichotomous image. Being less skilled reduced

Table 1

Distribution of Respondents with Respect to the Number of Social Classes Perceived, by Occupational Group

Occupational group	Number of social classes perceived		One class or no classes perceived	N
	Two	Three or more		
	Percentages			
Professionals and managers	25.8	69.0	5.2	97
Technicians and office workers	29.2	62.5	8.3	72
Skilled workers	43.6	48.7	7.7	78
Unskilled workers	40.0	38.2	21.8	55
Total	33.3	57.0	9.7	302

the probability that a respondent would distinguish more than two classes (38.2% compared to 48.7%); more of the same group, however, did not perceive the existence of any classes (21.8% compared to 7.7%).

Unskilled laborers are the one category where multi-class images of society are less common than two-class images. Concomitant with an increase in occupational status is a preference for an image of at least three classes (cf. Table 1).

The lower-class preference for a two-class depiction of social structure, along with the relative avoidance of such an image by the upper classes, is a finding consistent with the results of research carried out in several capitalist countries (Safilos-Rothschild, 1967; Lopreato and Hazelrigg, 1972; Lowe, 1977). Sometimes this pattern is interpreted as the effect of schooling.

To a certain degree, a person's educational level can be treated as an indicator of intellectual capacity. Yet Table 2 indicates that for a high-school level of education, the proportion of manual workers adopting a dichotomous image is nearly twice as great as for the corresponding proportion of white-collar workers.[2] Thus the propensity of manual workers to adopt more frequently a

Table 2

Proportion of Those Members of the Intelligentsia and the Working Class Who Hold a Dichotomous Class Image, by Education

Education	Intelligentsia	Working Class
	Percentages	
Elementary	0.0	44.1
Incomplete secondary	33.3	51.1
Secondary	24.2	44.1
College and above	28.2	0.0

dichotomous image of social structure cannot be explained by their lower education.

The difference in orientation between blue-collar and white-collar workers persists even after we introduce into the analysis variables characterizing economic conditions, such as earnings and per capita family income. Only members of the intelligentsia with extremely low incomes tend frequently to perceive a dichotomous social structure. Among manual workers, income level does not influence the appearance of a dichotomous image. This finding reveals that despite marked economic differentiation among Warsaw respondents there is no observable tendency for the better-paid workers to become similar to the intelligentsia in terms of class consciousness. The "labor aristocracy" adopts a dichotomous perspective just as often as do all other workers.

The role of other indicators of living conditions was also explored. Extreme deprivation in an individual's housing needs was shown to promote the emergence of a dichotomous image of social structure: respondents who lived in apartments where total space per family member was less than seven square meters were twice as prone as other individuals to see only two classes in society (74.2% compared to 32.5%). However, the rather small size of the sample made it impossible to control this systematically. It can only be concluded, therefore, that the category of persons with poor housing is differentiated in terms of other attributes of their social positions.

To summarize, class division (the working class as distinct from the intelligentsia) is related to the way social structure is perceived (a dichotomous image as opposed to other images). Attributes of social position (level of occupational skills, formal education, extreme deprivation in terms of housing) significantly influence the emergence of a dichotomous perspective across the entire sample. However, these variables do little to explain the mechanism by which the two social classes—workers and the intelligentsia—perceive social structure. Moreover, a dichotomous view of social structure is less dependent on individual attributes of social position in the case of working-class people than in the case of the intelligentsia.

"Roots" in the working-class environment

Our research has substantiated the well-documented thesis that a dichotomous image of society is characteristic of working-class consciousness (Hoggart, 1957; Popitz et al, 1969; Roberts et al, 1977). In this section we extend the thesis. We hope to show that being "rooted" in a working-class environment helps promote a tendency to distinguish social dichotomy. As indicators of working-class roots we adopt the following: (1) having a working-class father; (2) identifying with the working class; and (3) maintaining homogeneous class interaction with fellow workers.

While 58.2 percent of second-generation workers adopt a two-class image of society, only 38.5 percent of workers from peasant families and 31.8 percent of workers of intelligentsia origin do so. Within the entire working class the frequency of the dichotomous view has been reduced by the influx of individuals from other social classes. Manual workers of intelligentsia background perceive a dichotomous aspects of social structure only slightly more often than do members of their class of origin.

Table 3 presents the cumulative effect of the nature of work performed and subjective class identification on the adoption of a

Table 3

Proportion of Those Members of the Intelligensia and the Working Class Who Hold a Dichotomous Class Image, by Subjective Class Identification

Class self-identification	Intelligentsia	Working Class
	Percentages	
Intelligensia	17.9	37.5
Working class	26.3	48.2
Discriminated class	42.5	64.3
No identification	24.0	33.3

dichotomous view of the social structure. Comparing rows 2 and 4 in column 2, we notice that the likelihood of expressing a dichotomous view of social structure increases from one-third to nearly one-half when a worker identifies with his class. White-collar workers who regard themselves as members of the working class more often perceive a dichotomous society than do those who identify themselves with the intelligentsia. Moreover, by comparing the percentages given in column 1, rows 3 and 4, and column 2, rows 2 and 4, it can be seen that working-class identification increases the probability that a manual worker will perceive a social dichotomy to the same extent that identification with a discriminated class affects a white-collar worker.

The relationship between the individual and the collectivity is shaped by direct social contact. Through such interaction, the subculture of the group to which the individual belongs can be surmised. For this reason research on social consciousness often focuses on an individual's immediate social environment. A primary group is considered to be the critical variable intervening between the subculture and social consciousness (Bott, 1957; Lockwood, 1966). Our data permit us to verify whether the dichotomous class image is expressed more often by individuals whose close connection with the working-class subculture is produced by social contacts that are homogeneous with respect to class.

Table 4

Dichotomous Class Image by Type of Social Interaction

Variable	Percent of respondents holding a dichotomous class image	Kendall's Q
Formal contacts at work: Lack of informal contacts with superiors whose tasks differ from the respondent's	62.5	0.34
Informal contacts at work: Informal contacts with superiors whose tasks differ from the respondent's	65.5	0.43
Social contacts: Majority of friends are nonmanual workers	56.0	0.22

Table 4 reveals that identification of a dichotomous class image is more likely to occur when an individual enjoys homogeneous formal relations in his place of work and heterogenous informal relations at work and elsewhere. Workers more often adopt a dichotomous perspective if their link with the working-class milieu and their participation in the working-class subculture are achieved by means of personal ties with workmates. The probability of expressing a dichotomous class image is increased, however, when a worker is afforded the opportunity to relate observations about his own social class directly to the contrasting background he personally experiences through contacts with superiors at work or with friends. The non-working-class social milieu differs from the world of the working class. We assume that direct contacts with individuals outside one's group provide the basis for a specific "not-us" feeling.

The conclusion drawn from the data presented in this section is that an individual's connection with working-class culture promotes the internalization of a dichotomous view of society. Such a perspective is also generated when there is an opportunity to contrast one's own working-class experience with another culture. Crossing class barriers in everyday contacts compels the individual to make comparisons that often stimulate frustration. If this is so, such frustration can be interpreted as a sense of relative deprivation, which stimulates a dichotomous view of society.

Social mobility

The process of social mobility can be considered in terms of a broadening of an individual's perspectives—that is, of becoming knowledgeable about different social milieus. In line with this reasoning, socially mobile persons should be stimulated to perceive a fine partition of social structure.

A contrasting argument is that the number of social classes perceived by an individual represents an expression of his satisfaction or frustration with the fortunes that the reigning social order has meted out to him. Accordingly not all mobile persons adopt an image of a multilayer or multidimensional social structure: only those who have experienced social advancement subscribe to this view. Individuals who have suffered social demotion or deprivation, according to this argument, should opt for the dichotomous perspective because of its utility in expressing the conflictual nature of social relations.

The results presented in Table 5 help substantiate the satisfaction-frustration argument. Individuals whose occupational status is lower than that of their fathers are more than twice as likely to perceive social dichotomy as those who experienced intergenerational social advancement. The category of persons whose status approximates that of their fathers is not uniform in its perceptions: the stable intelligentsia view social structure in dichotomous terms about half as often as do stable workers. It is not so much the lack of upward mobility, therefore, that promotes a dichotomous class image, as it is a certain type of stability, namely, inheritance of the father's working-class position. Frustration produced by a decline in status or, in the case of stable workers, failure to increase status, also influences workers to adopt a dichotomous class image.

Table 5

Intergenerational Occupational Mobility and the Adoption of a Dichotomous Class Image[a]

Type of mobility	Percent of respondents holding a dichotomous class image
Upward	22.5
Immobility	39.2
Downward	46.1

[a]Occupational status was measured on the socioeconomic scale developed by Słomczyński and Kacprowicz (1979). The category of immobility includes those respondents whose status is lower or higher than the status of their fathers by no more than 20 points.

The experience of frustration is reinforced by the psychological climate of a "society of open recruitment" (a phrase applied to Poland in the 1970s; Narojek, 1980). This climate causes an individual to focus his attention on numerous instances of upward mobility. If one's own career stands in contrast to such successes, the feeling of failure is exacerbated. A growth in expectations over and above the system's capacity to satisfy them is likely to become a source of frustration, even for individuals who have achieved genuine advancement.

Dichotomous class image and support for radical change

The adoption of a dichotomous class image strengthens the individual's belief in the conflictual nature of existing social relations. Table 6 indicates the proportion of persons, classified by the manual/nonmanual nature of their work and by their class image, that can be labeled "radicals." Radicals are those who are convinced of the unjust nature of the present social order, its conflictual basis, and the clear need for change. The table shows that, when dichotomous class image is controlled for, the percent of radicals increases more than twofold among white-collar workers and more than threefold among manual workers. These relationships persisted, though not as strongly, when variables

Table 6

Proportion of Radicals by Nature of Work, and Number of Social Classes Distinguished during Two Interviews

Nature of work	Number of social classes	First interview	Second interview
		Percentages	
Nonmanual	Two	46.3	31.9
	Three or more	21.2	24.0
Manual	Two	29.2	22.2
	Three or more	9.4	14.0

concerned with social consciousness were measured at the end of a five-week interval.

Table 7 shows that nearly three-quarters of radical workers subscribe to a dichotomous class image, while slightly over one-third of the remaining workers adopt this outlook. A significant difference also emerges among white-collar workers divided into radicals and others (nearly one-half compared to one-fifth). Knowledge about an individual's radical beliefs helps to predict whether a dichotomous image will be adopted more in the case of manual workers than intelligentsia; the probability of making an error is .263 and .537 respectively.

When a worker talks of conflict and the need for change in the status quo, he simultaneously adopts a dichotomous image of social structure. Dichotomy serves as a useful tool for analyzing conflictual social relations. In a sense the radical worker is "dependent" on a dichotomous perspective. Such dependence means that in three out of four cases where radical attitudes toward the social order are expressed, the individual worker accepts a dichotomous viewpoint (Table 8). This dependence is also reflected in the fact that among workers avoiding a dichotomous class image, only every ninth one will subscribe to radical attitudes (Table 6). In contrast, the existence of radical views among

Table 7

Nature of Work, Type of Social Order Perceived, and the Adoption of a Dichotomous Class Image

Nature of work	Perception of social order	Percent of respondents holding a dichotomous class image
Nonmanual	Radical	46.3
	Other	19.6
Manual	Radical	73.7
	Other	34.7

white-collar workers is more often grounded in an image of social structure that rejects dichotomy. Accordingly, the radical member of the intelligentsia may avoid a dichotomous perspective more often than the radical manual worker.

The results presented in Table 8 lead us to following generalization: class images of blue-collar and white-collar workers would not differ if not for the existence of those blue-collar workers who perceive the social structuree in dichotomous terms. Manual workers thinking in these terms are distinguished from other groups by the relatively high degree of support for a program of social change consisting of three radical postulates: economic egalitarianism, workers' autonomy, and effective management.

For manual workers a dichotomous class image helps bring about a preference for a specific program of social change that strongly underscores economic equality. The proposal to redistribute of income is formulated in such a way that it almost recommends egalitarianism for its own sake. Similarly, the proposal for workers' autonomy is "pure": its growth is desired even where it might threaten a seldom questioned value, economic efficiency. This program also includes, finally, effective management; the alternative requires that society exercise control

Table 8

Nature of Work, Number of Social Classes Distinguished, and Affirmation of Postulates Regarding the Social Order

		Percent of respondents agreeing with postulates regarding the social order		
Nature of work	Number of social classes distinguished	"The highest earnings should be reduced, even if this would not lead to an increase in the lowest earnings."	"The influence of workers in the management of the factory should grow even at the cost of disruption of production."	"For authorities to avoid social unrest, it is imperative not to lose control of society."
Nonmanual	Two	34.0	22.0	19.5
	Three or more	25.0	23.0	16.0
Manual	Two	40.0	37.5	31.3
	Three or more	25.0	24.5	22.6

over government. Rejection of the alternative might originate not in a desire to eliminate the citizen's role as an "object" in dealing with the authorities, but rather in a wish to emphasize the responsibility the authorities incurred for the existing state of social affairs.[3]

The "ideology of social change" was still a program of the minority in 1979. In the entire sample more than two-thirds did not agree with an extreme version of egalitarianism; nearly three-quarters rejected the high price that would have to be paid for workers' autonomy; and in turn almost four-fifths would give priority to the "mechanism of democratic control" over the "effectiveness of government." Among manual workers sharing a dichotomous view of society, there was a tendency to view the desired social order in terms of a model usually described as monocentric. Workers supported "authorities who do not lose control over society" nearly as strongly as they did economic egalitarianism—an issue generally of great importance to them (Blachnicki, 1979; 102-3).

Conclusion

The manifestation of an aspect of social consciousness—the division of society into a given number of categories—has been shown to be an important variable because of its antecedents and consequences.

First, we observed that both "individual" and "group" factors promote the adoption of a dichotomous class image. The individual factors were conceived in terms of deprivation and the experience of frustration connected with downward mobility. The importance of group factors lies in the "roots" of the individual in a working-class community: a working-class identity, the inheritance of class affiliation from one's father, and a pattern of social interaction contributing to the sense of relative deprivation.

Second, we concluded that a dichotomous image of social structure has such consequences as shaping attitudes toward the prevailing social order, and a belief in the desirability of social change. However, we also observe the reciprocal relationship: persons recommending radical change are more inclined to adopt a dichotomous viewpoint than are other categories of respondents. Radical attitudes include demands for egalitarianism, management of enterprises by the labor force, and efficacious governing of the country. The readiness to divide social structure into a given number of categories is, accordingly, an essential link in the chain stretching from individual frustration and group affiliation to support for a change in the status quo. This conclusion is especially pertinent to the working class.

These empirical findings lead to some general reflections. The data collected in 1979—a time that, according to Stefan Nowak's "sociological calendar" (1981), ought to be classified as the end of the "latent phase" of sharp social conflict—indicate a significantly greater prevalence of a dichotomous class image and radical orientation than found in earlier studies (e.g. Słomczyński and Wesołowski, 1973; Borucki, 1975). The results of the Warsaw study therefore reflect a growing polarization of opinion about the prevailing social order; this polarization was documented in later studies (Adamski, 1982).

A comparison of the opinions obtained from the 1979 Warsaw sample with those of a 1980 national survey (Kolarska and Rychard 1982) leads to the following conclusion: in 1980 greater emphasis was placed on the redistribution of income and the role of self-management, while pressures for pluralism and for control over the activity of government were as strong as in 1979. The overall attitudes of society toward egalitarianism and workers' autonomy followed, in a sense, the path taken by the radical workers of Warsaw in 1979. The 1980 research (Kolarska and Rychard, 1982) indicated that, besides the pronounced support for a polycentric model of social order, there were also clear manifestations of acceptance of a monocentric model. The monocentric orientation was particularly strong among respondents whose social status is low, apparently substantiating the tendency noted in the 1979 study of Warsaw workers. This tendency persisted among manual workers who voiced a dichotomous class image, which is positively correlated with previous deprivation, roots in a working-class environment, and strong criticism of the existing social order. Monocentric tendencies emerged in the social consciousness of groups that were particularly destined to adopt radical collective action, given their psychological and organizational dispositions.

The Polish crisis of 1980 is generally viewed as having resulted from consensual and consistent social preferences and aspirations found either within the working class (Malanowski, 1981) or within the more broadly defined category of the "new middle class" (Kurczewski, 1982). Less attention has been paid to interclass differences. In this paper we have noted the existence of significant such differences: the preference of the working class for economic egalitarianism and self-management was much stronger than that of the intelligentsia. The intelligentsia displayed greater interest in control exercised by society over the authorities, while workers more often stressed the importance of effective government.

Notes

1. A detailed description of the technique employed and the typology constructed can be found in Zaborowski (1983). Intersubjective validity of radical attitudes was obtained by entrusting independent researchers with the task of interpreting respondents' answers. Accordingly, the final result is based on interpretations consensually agreed upon.
2. The average education of a blue-collar worker may be not equivalent to the average education of a white-collar worker because of differences in the types of schools attended or the course of an educational career.
3. The data suggest that the postulate of an "efficient government" did not have any "antidemocratic" connotations. This becomes clear when we observe that only 9 percent of respondents agreed with the idea of "limiting citizen rights for a longer period of time." The concept of "responsibility of the authorities for the state of the social order" is appropriate in this context in that such responsibility is usually related to the "maintenance of control" as well as to the methods used to achieve it. One interpretation is that this postulate involves "control of society" as opposed to "disorder," and that, accordingly, it is not an indiscriminate preference for all monocentric solutions.

References

Adamski, W.
    1982   "Structural and generational aspects of a social conflict." *Sisyphus* 3:49–58.
Blachnicki, B.
    1979   *Pracownicy przemysłu wobec egalitaryzmu*. [Industrial Employees and Egalitarianism.] Wrocław: Ossolineum.
Borucki, A.
    1975   "Struktura społeczna w świadomości mieszkańców Łodzi." [Social structure in the consciousness of Łódź residents.] Pp. 380–97 in Z. Bokszański, J. Kulpińska, and J. Woskowski (eds.), *Współczesna polska klasa robotnicza*. [Contemporary Polish Working Class.] Warsaw: Książka i Wiedza.
Bott, E.
    1957   *Family and Social Network*. London: Tavistock.
Cohen, E.
    1968   "Social images in an Israeli development town." *Human Relations* 21:163–76.
Hiller, P.

1975 "Nature and social locations of class." *Sociology* 9:1-28.
Hoggart, P.
1957 *The Uses of Literacy. Changing Patterns in English Mass Culture.* Fair Lawn, N.J.: Essential Books.
Kolarska, L. and A. Rychard
1982 "Vision of social order." *Sisyphus* 3:206-23.
Kurczewski, J.
1982 "The old system and the revolution." *Sisyphus* 3:21-32.
Lewis, L. S.
1964 "Class and the perception of class." *Social Forces* 42:336-40.
Lockwood, D.
1966 "Sources of variation of working class images of a society." *Sociological Review* 14:249-67.
Lopreato, J. and L. Hazelrigg
1972 *Class Conflict and Mobility.* San Francisco: Chandler.
Lowe, R.
1977 "Class images, social stratification and social mobility." Paper presented at the meeting of the Research Committee on Social Stratification of the International Sociological Association. Dublin, Ireland. 5-7 April.
Malanowski, J.
1981 *Polscy robotnicy.* [Polish Workers.] Warsaw: Książka i Wiedza.
Moorhouse, H. F.
1976 "Attitudes to class relationships in Britain." *Sociology* 10:469-96.
Narojek, W.
1980 *Społeczeństwo otwartej rekrutacji.* [Society of Open Recruitment.] Warsaw: Polish Scientific Publishers.
Nowak, S.
1981 "Dylemat więźnia." [Prisoner's dilemma.] Paper presented at the 6th Polish Sociological Congress. Łódź.
Ossowski, S.
1963 *Class Structure in the Social Consciousness.* New York: Macmillan.
Popitz, H., H. P. Bahrdt, E. A. Jüres, and A. Kesting
1969 "Workers' image of society." Pp. 281-324 in T. Burns (ed.), *Industrial Man.* Harmondsworth, Middlesex: Penguin.
Roberts, K., F. G. Cook, S. C. Clark, and E. Semeonoff
1977 *The Fragmentary Class Structure.* London: Heinemann.
Safilos-Rotschild, C.
1967 "Class position and success stereotypes in Greek and American cultures." *Social Forces* 45:374-82.
Słomczyński, K. M. and G. Kacprowicz
1979 *Skale zawodów.* [Occupational Scales.] Warsaw: Institute of Philosophy and Sociology of the Polish Academy of Sciences.
Słomczyński, K. M. and W. Wesołowski
1973 "Potoczna percepcja struktury klasowej." [Everyday perception

of class structure.] Pp. 241-69 in K. M. Słomczyński and W. Wesołowski (eds.), *Struktura i ruchliwość społeczna.* [Social Structure and Mobility.] Wrocław: Ossolineum.

Słomczyński, K. M., M. Soszyńska, and W. Zaborowski
1977 "Potoczna percepcja struktury społecznej: jej uwarunkowania i konsekwencje." [Everyday perception of social structure: its determinants and consequences.] Pp. 82-99 in W. Wesołowski and E. Wnuk-Lipiński (eds.), *Projekty badawcze. Problem 11.2.* [Research Projects. Problem 11.2.] Warsaw: Institute of Philosophy and Sociology of the Polish Academy of Sciences.

Tumin, M. K. and A. Feldman
1961 *Social Class and Social Change in Puerto Rico.* Princeton, N.J.: Princeton University Press.

Westergaard, J. and H. Resler
1975 *Class in a Capitalist Society. A Study of Contemporary Britain.* London: Heinemann.

Zaborowski, W.
1983 "Percepcja struktury społecznej i obrazy dystrybucji dóbr." [Perception of social structure and images of distribution of goods.] Unpublished. Ph.D. dissertation. Institute of Sociology of the University of Warsaw.

The Subjective Evaluation of Social Status

KAZIMIERZ M. SŁOMCZYŃSKI and GRAŻYNA KACPROWICZ

Introduction

Interest in how individuals perceive their place in the social structure originated with the theoretical proposition that the political views of persons who identify with the working class are different from the views of persons who identify with other social classes (Centers, 1949). This proposition underlies a number of studies in the United States and Western Europe in which self-identification with the working class is contrasted with self-identification with the middle class (e.g. Buchanan and Cantril, 1953; Hamilton, 1966; Lopreato and Hazelrigg, 1972; for a review see Zaborowski, 1981). In almost all research on class identification, social classes are treated as distinctive and recognized human collectivities; classes are equated with social groups having different ways of life, behavior patterns, norms, and the like.[1]

The theoretical point of departure of this paper is that social structure can be understood not only in terms of social classes, but also in terms of social strata as determined by the unequal distribution of goods and values. Researchers considering the distribu-

---

This research was supported by the Institute of Philosophy and Sociology of the Polish Academy of Sciences, and by the Institute of Sociology of the University of Warsaw. The authors are indebted to Krystyna Janicka for her participation in planning and administering the study. Bruce Roberts provided computer assistance.

tive aspect of social structure in social consciousness need to examine how individuals perceive their place along the continuum of social status. Thus, the subjective evaluation of social status refers not to class divisions but to layers of the stratification system (Morris and Murphy, 1966; Słomczyński, 1969).[2]

In Poland, studies on the evaluation of social status have been frequently undertaken and they are now a mainstay in the repertoire of empirical social research (e.g. Sarapata, 1965; Nowak, 1966; Borucki, 1967; Tobera, 1972; Słomczyński, 1972; Słomczyński and Wesołowski, 1973; Święcicka, 1980). Interview schedules designed for use with large representative samples often contain a question on how highly the respondent evaluates his or her social status on a five- or seven-point ordinal scale. Although survey design differs among the studies, they all aim at obtaining a self-evaluation of social status based on answers to a single question. Thus, a straightforward synthetic measurement procedure has been applied in these studies.

To measure the subjective evaluation of social status we utilize an analytical measurement procedure, also called inferential. This procedure is based on the assumption that the overall status evaluation may be expressed as a function of self-appraisals of status components, such as income, education, participation in decision-making, or prestige. These specific self-appraisals are treated as indicators, that is, observable variables. Overall status evaluation is inferred from these indicators and is conceived of as a latent variable.

The question as to whether the analytical approach should replace the synthetic approach in measuring the evaluation of social status needs to be addressed empirically. In our opinion the analytical approach is theoretically better justified, while the synthetic approach is easier to use in survey applications. After describing the analytical approach in some detail we devote a part of this paper to a comparison of the results obtained by utilizing both approaches. A new interpretation of the results obtained by employing the synthetic approach is offered.

A large part of our analysis focuses on the determinants and correlates of the subjective evaluation of social status. In particular, we are concerned with those determinants that constitute the most important elements of objective social status: education, occupation, and income. The main research question is: to what extent does objective social status determine its subjective evaluation?

Data

Data are from surveys conducted in Łódź in 1967, 1976, and 1980. In each of those years a sample of men aged 21 to 65 who were heads of families and working in civilian occupations was interviewed. Probability samples of about 1,000 persons were drawn from census data of the city's inhabitants. The distribution of basic demographic variables was found to be unbiased. At each time point the relationship of education, occupation, and income was similar to that in other large Polish cities.

The interview schedule contained questions about the evaluation of social status in terms of seven criteria: education, occupational skills, nature of work (manual vs. nonmanual), authority (influence on management decision making), social prestige, income, and the consumption of cultural goods. The core question read: "How do you evaluate your position in society as compared with that of other people, when various aspects of it are considered? Let's start with education. In terms of education, do you hold a much higher, higher, or slightly higher position than average? Or, is your position average, slightly below average, lower, or much lower than average?" Once the respondent had answered the question concerning education, he was asked about his position on the other dimensions of social differentiation. In addition he was asked about the overall evaluation of his social status.

The multiple indicator model
of evaluation of social status

Table 1 presents distributions of self-appraisals of status components in the 1967 and 1980 surveys. To perform quantitative analysis we assigned consecutive natural numbers to particular answers; the assigned numbers ranged from 1 for very low evaluation to 7 for very high evaluation. These scores were compared with scores obtained from fitting the original distribution to the normal and to the log-normal distributions. The natural number scores and the scores of both transformed scales produced nearly identical results because of very strong correlations ($r \geq 0.95$). Thus, for further analyses we have chosen the natural number scores, with distances between adjacent categories assumed constant.

Self-appraisals in 1980 are similar to those made thirteen years earlier. The ordering of the arithmetic means of the scores is the same for both surveys: the highest value is obtained by occupational skills, followed by prestige, nature of work, income, education, consumption of cultural goods, and, finally, participation in management. In 1980, however, self-appraisals were systematically lower than in 1967. A particularly visible decline in self-appraisal occurred in the case of participation in management: 38.2 percent of respondents assessed their participation as low in 1967; in 1980 this percent rose to 61.3.

Table 2 shows the correlations between self-appraisals. The mean value of these correlations is .364 for 1967 while it is .303 for 1980. It is surprising that for all r we have $r_{1967} > r_{1980}$. We surmise that the economic and political crisis emerging in Poland at the beginning of 1980 weakened the relationship between self-appraisals according to various criteria. This conjecture is supported by the fact that the 1976 findings are more similar to those of 1967 than to those of 1980.

Correlations among self-appraisals are used in a confirmatory factor analysis contained in the LISREL (Jöreskog and Sörbom, 1978) and MILS (Schoenberg, 1981) programs.[3] Figure 1 presents a measurement model of the subjective evaluation of social status expressed in the notation of these two programs. This is an *a priori* model which appeared to have been substantively justified. We assumed that the variables describing the evaluation of social

Table 1

Distribution of Answers to the Questions about Self-evaluation of Social Status in Terms of Specific Criteria (Łódź 1967 and 1980)

Criteria of evaluation	Evaluations in percentages			Arithmetic mean[c]	Standard deviation[c]
	low[a]	average	high[b]		
A. 1980 study					
Education	31.9	50.4	15.8	3.68	1.15
Occupational skills	10.1	42.1	45.8	4.57	1.17
Nature of work	18.4	52.4	23.9	4.05	1.15
Participation in management	61.3	22.4	11.3	2.61	1.53
Social prestige	15.4	64.9	31.4	4.24	1.23
Income	27.8	57.5	13.1	3.72	0.97
Consumption of cultural goods	40.1	41.5	15.9	3.49	1.39
B. 1967 study					
Education	30.0	51.1	18.6	3.79	1.17
Occupational skills	10.1	42.1	47.3	4.61	1.17
Nature of work	16.6	44.8	26.8	4.32	1.25
Participation in management	38.2	33.6	24.0	3.58	1.55
Social prestige	10.6	42.0	45.1	4.58	1.22
Income	25.2	56.1	18.4	3.81	1.09
Consumption of cultural goods	27.1	37.7	33.2	3.74	1.28

[a]The sum of answers: "very low," "low," and "slightly lower than average."
[b]The sum of answers: "very high," "high," and "slightly higher than average."
[c]Scores from 1, for "very low," to 7, for "very high."

status should reflect three dimensions: knowledge, work, and rewards. These dimensions correspond to three dimensions of objective social status whose indentification has been confirmed in another study (Słomczyński, 1983). In this version of the model, education and occupational skills are indicators of knowledge; the nature of work and participation in management define the work dimension; income, social prestige, and consumption of cultural goods correspond to the dimension of rewards. However, this version of the model was deemed unacceptable: first, because

Table 2

Correlations among Self-evaluations of Social Status in Terms of Seven Criteria. Łódź 1967—below the Main Diagonal; Łódź 1980—above the Main Diagonal

Criterion of evaluation	(1)	(2)	(3)	(4)	(5)	(6)	(7)
(1) Education	1.000	.338	.372	.343	.216	.325	.373
(2) Occupational skills	.409	1.000	.469	.270	.339	.272	.170
(3) Nature of work	.470	.530	1.000	.334	.349	.370	.272
(4) Participation in management	.425	.369	.459	1.000	.332	.292	.281
(5) Social prestige	.270	.369	.350	.385	1.000	.223	.200
(6) Income	.458	.318	.407	.341	.229	1.000	.208
(7) Consumption of cultural goods	.389	.239	.274	.357	.330	.275	1.000

the estimates obtained gave poor goodness of fit, and, second, because some parameters were statistically insignificant. Therefore, the model was modified using the diagnostic part of MILS program.

In the final version of our model the nature of work, participation in management, and social prestige define the occupational dimension of status. After it was discovered that social prestige is a statistically insignificant indicator of "rewards," we decided to regroup the indicators. Since this variable was strongly correlated with the nature of work and participation in management, we assume that it also reflects occupation. The fact that social prestige is apparently understood by respondents in the context of occupational characteristics has been reported in the literature (Sarapata, 1965; Słomczyński, 1972). In order to avoid confusion we shall use the term "occupational dimension" instead of "work dimension."

Table 3 gives estimated parameters of the final version of the model for studies conducted in Łódź in 1967, 1976, and 1980. All values of the path coefficients are statistically significant ($p \leq .05$). With the exception of self-appraisal of income in 1976, the inter-study differences between the values of the path coefficients

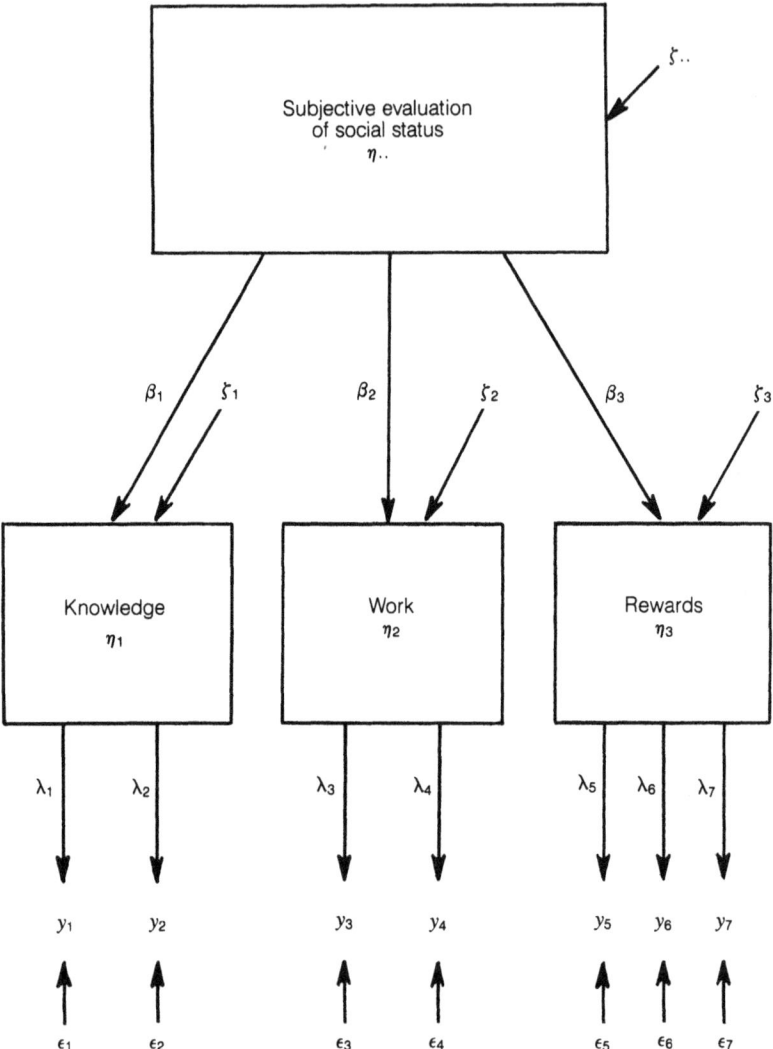

Figure 1. A priori measurement model of the subjective evaluation of social status.

The variables y denote answers to the questions about the evaluation of status is terms of education (y_1), occupational skills (y_2), nature of work (y_3), participation in management (y_4), social prestige (y_5), income (y_6), and cultural consumption (y_7). The λs are path coefficients from unobserved constructs η to observed variables y while the ε are residual values of observed variables. The regression coefficients β and the residual values ζ define the unobserved constructs η.

Table 3

Confirmatory Factor Analysis of the Subjective Evaluation of Social Status (Łódź 1980, 1976, and 1967)

Constructs and indicators	1980 study	1976 study	1967 study
	Path coefficients[a]		
A. Relationships between constructs and indicators			
Knowledge			
Education	.768	.725	.694
Occupational skills	.445	.509	.593
Occupation			
Nature of work	.639	.689	.718
Participation in management	.576	.592	.642
Social prestige	.474	.501	.523
Rewards			
Income	.521	.391	.609
Sharing in cultural goods	.427	.504	.420
B. Relationships between constructs			
Overall status			
Knowledge	.954	.963	.971
Occupation	.824	.901	.922
Rewards	.949	.952	.968
Ratio of χ^2 to the degrees of freedom	3.2	3.8	2.7

[a] All values statistically significant ($p \leq .05$).

for the same self-appraisals are rather small. Therefore, we conclude that the three-dimensional representation of evaluation of social status is stable over time. Also stable are the values of the coefficients of regression of the higher-order construct—global evaluation of status—on the lower-order constructs, that is, evaluation of knowledge, occupation, and rewards. In each study, global evaluation of social status reflects its knowledge dimension most strongly and its rewards dimension least strongly.

The measurement model gives an adequate representation of the data in terms of the goodness of fit. The ratio of the chi-square statistic to the number of degrees of freedom is below 3.8. Sub-

Table 4

Correlation and Regression of Self-evaluation of Social Status with Education, Occupation, and Income (Łódź 1980)

Criterion of evaluation	Correlation			Regression[a]			Multiple correlation[b]
	Education	Occupation	Income	Education	Occupation	Income	
(1) Education	.659	.521	.217	.580	.103	.016	.663
(2) Occupational skills	.332	.351	.243	.119	.226	.144	.391
(3) Nature of work	.323	.330	.228	.153	.184	.131	.374
(4) Participation in management	.240	.249	.195	.104	.140	.126	.290
(5) Social prestige	.115	.165	.091	.016	.163	.050	.172
(6) Income	.257	.253	.408	.086	.092	.357	.437
(7) Consumption of cultural goods	.338	.285	.126	.270	.086	.022	.344

[a] Regression of self-appraisal according to a given criterion on education, occupation, and income.
[b] Correlation of self-appraisal according to a given criterion with three variables: education, occupation, and income.

stantively, the application of inferential measurement to the evaluation of social status, which has resulted in the educational, occupational, and rewards dimensions, is consistent with the sociological tradition of the multidimensional approach to social stratification. The structure of the model is new in comparison with the structure of multiple indicator models of class identification (e.g. Sörbom and Jöreskog, 1978; Jackman and Jackman, 1973; Kluegel et al., 1977).

The impact of education, occupation, and income on the subjective evaluation of social status

Table 4 presents the coefficients of regression of the self-appraisal of status components on three objective variables: education, occupation, and income. In this analysis, education is expressed by the number of years of schooling; occupation is measured on the scale of socioeconomic rewards (Słomczyński and Kacprowicz, 1979); and, income is given in złotys of monthly earnings. We assume that schooling corresponds to the knowledge dimension of objective social status, while the two remaining objective variables correspond to the occupational and reward dimensions.

Self-appraisal of education is most strongly determined by the number of years of schooling and self-appraisal of occupational skills according to the socioeconomic index. In the latter case, however, the gross effect of the number of years of schooling is relatively high ($r = .322$), and its reduction after controlling for the socio-economic index and income is far from complete ($\beta = .119$). The amount of monthly earnings from one's job most strongly determines self-appraisal of income. The socioeconomic index most strongly determines self-appraisal of the nature of work, followed by participation in management, and social prestige. This result provides additional justification for incorporating self-appraisal of social prestige into the occupational dimension. Moreover, we conclude that correspondence between the objective and subjective dimensions of status exists, although it is not close.

The last column of Table 4 shows the combined impact of education, occupation, and income on the self-evaluation of social status in terms of particular criteria. In the optimal situation, the three objective variables explain about 45 percent of the variance of the subjective variable; this is the case for self-appraisal of education. In the remaining cases the percent of explained variance is much lower; it ranges between 3 and 20. In studies from 1967 and 1976 these values are even lower. We need to consider to what extent these small effects of particular self-appraisals are cumulative. Is the combined impact of education, occupation, and income on overall status self-evaluation also weak?

Figure 2 presents the causal model in which objective social status determines its subjective evaluation. In this model we sought to retain the analogy between dimensions of objective

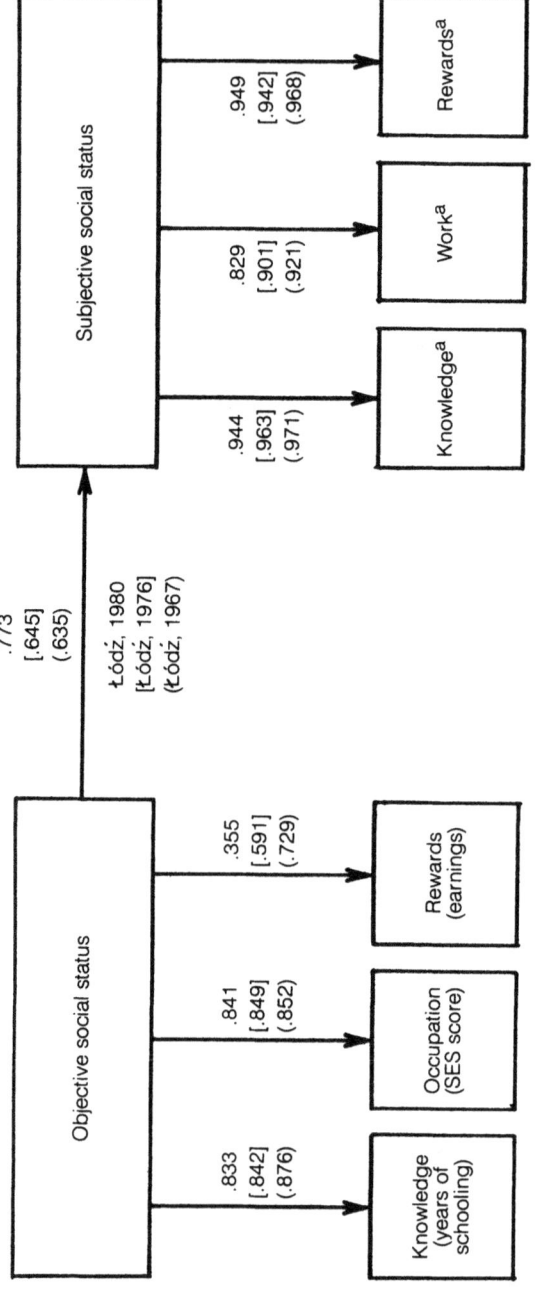

Figure 2. Relationship between objective and subjective social status.
[a]For a measurement model see Table 3

status and its perception. In both objective status and its perception we distinguished the educational, occupational, and rewards dimensions.

For describing objective social status the education and socioeconomic index are important and stable for the period 1967-80. The values of the path coefficients of corresponding constructs are very high and do not change across studies ($.833 \leq \beta \leq .876$). By contrast, the importance of income decreases over time; the value of the path coefficient for that variable is .729 for 1967 and .355 for 1980. In the late 1970s the correlation of income with both education and occupation weakened. In this sense the increase in status inconsistency continued (Słomczyński and Wesołowski, 1978).

Generally, objective social status determines subjective self-evaluation to a very substantial degree. It explains from about 40 percent (in 1967 and 1976) to about 60 percent (in 1980) of the variance of self-evaluation. This increase in determination demonstrates that during a social crisis perception of one's own place in the social structure becomes more realistic.

The synthetic measurement of subjective evaluation of social status: A new interpretation

Thus far we have been concerned with the analytic procedure for measuring the subjective evaluation of social status; we inferred the overall evaluation from a set of indicators. As was pointed out in the introduction, the traditional procedure is different; it is based on answers to a single question. Can the result of such a simplified measurement be presented as a function of self-appraisals of status components? Does it display as strong a relationship with the objective factors of social position as it does in the case of inferential measurement?

Table 5 shows the correlations between the synthetic measure of self-evaluation of social status and self-appraisals in terms of particular criteria. In both the 1967 and 1980 surveys the highest

Table 5

Correlation between Self-appraisals of Status Components and Overall Status Evaluation Obtained as an Answer to a Single Question (Łódź 1980 and 1967)

Criteria of evaluation	Overall evaluation of social status	
	1980 study	1967 study
Education	.429	.402
Occupational skills	.274	.297
Nature of work	.359	.363
Participation in management	.292	.282
Social prestige	.260	.258
Income	.400	.352
Consumption of cultural goods	.217	.231
Multiple correlation[a]	.540	.521

[a]Correlation of overall self-evaluation of social status with all self-appraisals of status components.

correlations are recorded for self-appraisal of education, followed by self-appraisal of income and nature of work. In both studies we find that the lowest value occurs for self-appraisal of consumption of cultural goods.

All self-appraisals considered together explain less than 30 percent of the variance of the overall evaluation of social status given as answers to a single question. Moreover, the synthetic measure is weakly related to the inferential measure. The value of the correlation coefficient in the 1980 study is .491.

We do not claim that a single question about the evaluation of overall social status in the interview schedule gives biased results. We believe, however, that the interpretation of answers to this question should be undertaken not in terms of comparing one's own position with that of other people, but in terms of satisfaction related to the situations recognized by the respondents as desirable or expected. Data in Table 6 show that between 1976 and 1980 a decline was recorded in the average evaluation of the social status of all occupational groups with the exception

Table 6

Average Score of Overall Status Evaluation Obtained as an Answer to a Single Question, by Occupational Group (Łódź 1980, 1976, and 1967)

Occupational group	1980 study	1976 study	1967 study
Professionals	4.38	4.61	4.77
Office workers	4.08	4.29	4.27
Technicians	3.92	4.26	4.28
Foremen	3.84	4.19	4.23
Craftsmen	3.66	4.01	4.24
Service workers	3.78	3.86	3.98
Skilled workers	3.76	3.96	3.97
Unskilled workers	3.74	3.71	3.62

of unskilled workers. Since this decline is not reflected in the objective social position of occupational groups, it can be interpreted as a manifestation of discontent caused by a faster rate of growth in aspirations than in the improvement of objective conditions.

The relationship between answers to the question about the overall evaluation of social status on the one hand, and education, occupation, and income on the other, is the strongest in 1980. Since education, occupation, and income together explain no more than 13.6 percent of the variability of the answers to this question ($R \geq .368$), any suggestion that these answers reflect objective status does not appear justified.

The weak relationship between occupational category and level of education on the one hand, and answers to the question about overall evaluation of social status on the other, has not changed since the early 1960s. On the basis of an empirical study conducted in 1961, Sarapata (1965:339) concluded: "In the representative Łódź studies . . . it was found that occupational category and level of education are not very effective determinants of the subjective evaluation of one's own social status. . . . The effects of these two variables are not additive and people from the same occupational category but on different levels of education found themselves on the same rung of the status ladder." More than twenty years later the conclusion still holds. However, this conclusion is not applicable to the subjective evaluation of social status measured by the analytical procedure. We have already shown that objective status strongly determines its subjective evaluation, which is inferred from self-appraisals of the status components.

Discussion and conclusion

In this paper we have presented a multiple-indicator model of the subjective evalution of social status. The model was constructed on the basis of answers to a battery of questions in which respondents were asked to evaluate their social position in terms of education, occupational skills, nature of work (manual/nonmanual), participation in management, social prestige, income, and consumption of cultural goods. The application of a confirmatory factor analysis led to the distinguishing of three dimensions of social status evaluation: knowledge, occupation, and rewards. Self-appraisal of education and occupational skills represent *a priori* selected indicators of the knowledge dimension. Self-appraisal of the nature of work, participation in management, and social prestige define the occupational dimension. Finally, the rewards dimension was inferred from self-appraisal of income and consumption of cultural goods. In general, this three-dimensional model fits the data very well. It is justified since it corresponds to everyday perceptions of the distribution of goods and values.

The analytical procedure for measuring the evaluation of social status makes it possible to study subjectively understood status inconsistency. Research on its psychological consequences generally takes into account differences between an individual's position along objectively defined "dimensions" of this position. Our multivariate measurement model contains a subjectively depicted localization of individuals along three dimensions: knowledge, occupation, and rewards. Does the subjectively perceived disparity of status factors reinforce the negative consequences of the objectively existing disparity in status factors? To what extent does the lack of equilibrium in the evaluation of status components engender a need for a change in objective conditions, particularly in improving those factors that were evaluated as being at a low level? These are examples of issues which further analysis could address empirically.

An important goal in methodological studies would be to improve the way questions about the evaluation of social status are formulated in interview schedules. The main reservation about the questions used in our study is the lack of a natural standard of comparing categories of answers on a common scale. First, for a given respondent the distance between "very high status" and "high status" may be different from the distance between "very low status" and "low status." Second, for two individuals the distance between the same pair of categories of answers may not be the same. One possible solution would be to ask the respondent what proportion of people are higher or lower in status than he. A common scale is embedded in this formulation of the question.

The correlation between objective social status, measured by education (number of years of schooling), occupation (socioeconomic index), and income (monthly salary from one's job), and its global subjective evaluation was stable during the period 1967–1976 ($.635 \leq r \leq .645$). Between 1976 and 1980 this correlation increased significantly ($r_{1980} - r_{1976} = .128$). In consequence, at the beginning of the 1980s the variables defining objective social status explained about sixty percent of the variance in its subjective evaluation. In Poland, the proportion of people who subjectively evaluate their social status by referring to objective criteria is no smaller than in advanced capitalist countries, the United States in particular.

One of the major findings of this paper is that the synthetic measure of the subjective evaluation of social status, obtained by means of answers to a single question, does not provide an adequate representation of self-appraisals of status components. The relationship between answers to the question about the overall evaluation of social status on the one hand, and answers to the questions about self-appraisals according to single criteria are—at most—modest ($.217 \leq r \leq .429$). We have confidence in this result, since these relationships fluctuate little accross surveys ($.004 \leq r_{1980} - r_{1976} \leq .048$). In addition, the synthetic measure is weakly correlated with the analytical measure and cannot be treated as a substitute for the evaluation of social status in terms of distribution of goods and values. The synthetic measure does not offer interpretations that identify the dimensions of the stratification system embedded in social consciousness.

In analyses of the subjective evaluation of social status based on answers to a single question, it was found that factors such as education, occupation, and income influence the evaluations. Nowak (1966:88) observed: "These factors can complement, replace or offset each other in their effects, forming something in the nature of a synthetic, subjective social ladder. Taken together they account for a significant part of variability in evaluations of social status." In our surveys, education, occupation, and income explain less than 15 percent of the variance in the overall evaluation of the synthetically measured social status of an individual. The quoted assertion holds less strongly for the synthetic than for the analytical measurement procedure. Indeed, the relationship of objective status with its subjective evaluation, inferred from self-appraisals of status components, is substantial ($r \geq .6$).

Notes

1. In Poland research on class identification focuses on two large categories: the "working class" and the "intelligentsia" (e.g. Janicki and Widerszpil, 1959; Malanowski, 1967; Lutyńska, 1965; Święcicki, 1980); both of these categories are interpreted in class-related terms.

2. Although the distinction between class structure and the stratification system is deeply rooted in sociological tradition, it is still controversial; see Mach and Wesołowski (1982). We assume that the stratification system consists of hierarchically ordered statuses; subjective evaluation of status is a part of "status awareness," which reflects "the ability on the part of the members of a society to place self and others on . . . status continuum" (Morris and Murphy, 1966:279).

3. Confirmatory factor analysis serves to test hypotheses about whether a given set of indicators can be reduced to a smaller number of latent variables. A description of this kind of factor analysis is found in Jöreskog (1969) and Sörbom and Jöreskog (1978); see also Long (1976) and Carmines and McIver (1981).

References

Borucki, A.
    1967   *Kariery zawodowe i postawy społeczne inteligencji w PRL w 1945–1959.* [Occupational Careers and Social Attitudes of Intelligentsia in P(olish) P(eople's) R(epublic) from 1945 to 1959.] Wrocław: Ossolineum.

Buchanan, W. and H. Cantril
    1953   *How Nations See Each Other.* Urbana, Ill.: University of Illinois Press.

Carmines, E. G. and J. P. McIver
    1981   "Analyzing models with unobserved variables: analysis of covariance structures." Pp. 136–98 in G. W. Bohrnstedt and E. Borgatta (eds.), *Social Measurement: Current Issues.* Beverly Hills: Sage.

Centers, R.
    1949   *The Psychology of Social Classes.* Princeton, N.J. Princeton University Press.

Hamilton, R. F.
    1966   "The marginal middle class: a reconsideration." *American Sociological Review* 31:192–9.

Jackman, R. R. and R. W. Jackman
    1973   "An interpretation of the relation between objective and subjective social status." *American Sociological Review* 38:569–82.

Janicki, J. and S. Widerszpil
    1959   "Do jakiej klasy należysz?" ["To which class do you belong?"] *Życie Gospodarcze* 405(25) and 407(27).

Jöreskog, K. G.
    1969   "A general approach to confirmatory maximum likelihood factor analysis." *Psychometrika* 34: 185–202.

Jöreskog, K. G. and D. Sörbom
    1978   *LISREL IV—A General Computer Program for Estimation of a Linear Structural System by Maximum Likelihood Methods.* Chicago, Ill.: International Educational Services.

Kluegel, J. R., R. Singleton, and C. E. Starnes
    1977   "Subjective class identification: a multiple indicator approach." *American Sociological Review* 42:599–611.

Long, J. S.
    1976   "Estimation and hypothesis testing in linear models containing error: a review of Jöreskog's model for the analysis of covariance

structures." *Sociological Methods and Research* 5:157-206.
Lopreato, J. and L. Hazelrigg
   1972   *Class Conflict, and Mobility.* San Francisco: Chandler.
Lutyńska, K.
   1965   *Pozycja społeczna urzędników w Polsce Ludowej.* [Social Position of Office Workers in People's Poland.] Wrocław: Ossolineum.
Mach, B. and W. Wesołowski
   1982   *Ruchliwość a teoria struktury społecznej.* [Mobility and the Theory of Social Structure.] Warsaw: Polish Scientific Publishers.
Malanowski, J.
   1967   *Stosunki klasowe i różnice społeczne w mieście.* [Class Relationships and Social Differences in a City.] Warsaw: Polish Scientific Publishers.
Morris, R. and R. Murphy
   1966   "A paradigm for the study of class consciousness." *Sociology and Social Research* 50:297-313.
Nowak, S.
   1966   "Psychologiczne aspekty przemian struktury społecznej i ruchliwości społecznej" [Psychological aspects of change in social structure and mobility.] *Studia Socjologiczne* No. 2:75-107.
Sarapata, A.
   1965   *Studia nad uwarstwieniem i ruchliwością społeczną w Polsce.* [Studies on Social Stratification and Mobility in Poland.] Warsaw: Książka i Wiedza.
Schoenberg, R.
   1981   *Documentation for MILS (Multiple Indicator Linear Structural Models).* Bethesda, Md.: National Institute of Mental Health.
Słomczyński, K. M.
   1983   *Pozycja zawodowa i jej związki z wykształceniem.* [Occupational Status and Its Relation to Education.] Warsaw: Institute of Philosophy and Sociology of the Polish Academy of Sciences.
   1972   *Zróżnicowanie społeczno-zawodowe i jego korelaty.* [Socio-occupational Differentiation and Its Correlates.] Wrocław: Ossolineum.
   1969   "Theoretical, methodological, and empirical problems of class-stratum identification." *Polish Round Table* 3:133-46.
Słomczyński, K. M. and G. Kacprowicz
   1979   *Skale zawodów.* [Scales of Occupations.] Warsaw: Institute of Philosophy and Sociology of the Polish Academy of Sciences.
Słomczyński, K. M. and W. Wesołowski
   1978   "Reduction of social inequalities and status inconsistency." Pp. 103-21 in Polish Sociological Association (ed.), *Social Structure—Polish Sociology 1977.* Wrocław: Ossolineum.
   1973   "Potoczna percepcja struktury społecznej." [Common perception of social structure.] Pp. 241-69 in K. M. Słomczyński and W. Wesołowski (eds.), *Struktura i ruchliwość społeczna.* [Social Structure and Mobility.] Wrocław: Ossolineum.

Sörbom, D. and K. G. Jöreskog
   1978   "The use of LISREL in sociological model building." Ninth World Congress of Sociology. Uppsala, Sweden. August 14-18.

Święcicka, M.
   1980   "Samoocena pozycji społecznej inteligencji." [Self-appraisal of social status by the intelligentsia.] Pp. 77-95 in A. Borucki (ed.), *Polska inteligencja współczesna: z problematyki samowiedzy.* [The Contemporary Polish Intelligentsia: Problems of Self-consciousness.] Warsaw: The Institute of Philosophy and Sociology of the Polish Academy of Sciences.

Święcicki, W.
   1980   "Samoidentyfikacja inteligencji na tle postrzeganej struktury społecznej." [Self-identification of the intelligentsia within a perceived pattern of social stratification.] Pp. 57-75 in A. Borucki (ed.), *Polska inteligencja współczesna: z problematyki samowiedzy.* [The Contemporary Polish Intelligentsia: Problems of Self-consciousness.] Warsaw: Institute of Philosophy and Sociology of the Polish Academy of Sciences.

Tobera, P.
   1972   *Zróżnicowanie społeczne pracowników przemysłu.* [Social Differentiation of Industrial Employees.] Warsaw: Polish Scientific Publishers.

Zaborowski, W.
   1981   "Potoczne wizje struktury społecznej i identyfikacje klasowe." [Common perceptions of social structure and class identification.] Pp. 149-79 in K. M. Słomczyński and W. Wesołowski (eds.), *Zróżnicowanie społeczne w perspektywie porównawczej.* [Social Differentiation in Comparative Perspective.] Wrocław: Ossolineum.

The Prestige of Education

ZBIGNIEW SAWIŃSKI

Introduction

The study of occupational prestige has a long tradition in empirical sociology. Treiman (1977) analyzed the results of research on occupational prestige conducted in sixty countries throughout the world. In Poland, over fifteen research projects have dealt with occupational prestige in the period 1958–79 (Pohoski, Słomczński and Wesołowski, 1976; Słomczyński and Kacprowicz, 1979). Findings have shown a basic similarity in the hierarchy of occupational prestige between Poland and other countries, and idiosyncratic Polish peculiarities have been explained (Sarapata and Wesołowski, 1961; Treiman, 1977; Wesołowski and Słomczyński, 1977). That the hierarchy of basic occupations according to prestige has a cross-cultural universality has been well substantiated by sociologists.

At the same time that empirical research on occupational prestige has expanded, numerous theoretical and methodological studies have also been published (for example, Goldthorpe and Hope, 1974; Blaikie, 1977; Sarapata, 1975). Without becoming engrossed in terminological controversies that have recently emerged, let us recall two fundamental principles: (1) the concept of prestige deals with occupational roles distinguished in terms of the division of labor; and (2) prestige is a form of

---

This empirical study was conducted by the Institute of Sociology of the University of Warsaw. The author wishes to thank Henryk Domański, Ewa Nasalska, and Magdalena Sawińska for helpful comments on an earlier version of the paper.

evaluation of occupational roles according to criteria that reflect the value systems of evaluators in a particular society. Prestige is, accordingly, a manifestation of social consciousness.

The method most often used to measure occupational prestige consists of presenting a respondent with a list of occupational titles (usually ranging from 10 to 100) and asking him or her to evaluate each title on a predetermined scale. The evaluations obtained are then aggregated into a unidimensional ranking; this ranking is treated as a hierarchy of occupations in terms of prestige.

We define *educational prestige* as the respect or esteem shown to persons who have a given level and type of education. Normally, three levels of education are recognized: primary, secondary, and tertiary. The type of education is identified with the type of school attended. We assume that the level and type of education is socially perceived as a dimension of social stratification, and as such constitutes a source of prestige.

Educational prestige is conceptually different from occupational prestige. Moreover, analyses of occupational differentiation in terms of prestige are based on the theory of the division of labor, which justifies distinguishing particular occupational roles to which prestige can be ascribed (Treiman, 1977). In the case of educational prestige, however, it is difficult to point to a theory that justifies the construction of analogous elementary categories that are not internally differentiated.

In this study we treat educational categories, which constitute the subject of evaluation in terms of prestige, as analytical. However, the problem as to which criteria should be employed to distinguish these categories remains. Is it sufficient to consider only the level of education, or should other factors be examined, such as the character of education (for example, medical or technical), types of studies (for youth or for adults who work), and types of schools (for example, high school or technical school)? Since this problem has not yet been theoretically resolved, we examine various criteria that have significance in the Polish educational system.

The current Polish educational system originated in the late

1940s and early 1950s. Elementary school consists of a compulsory eight-year program (seven years, until 1968). At the secondary-school level there are three different educational tracks and pupils in a particular track follow different programs of study from other tracks. These educational tracks include: (1) *vocational schools*, in which studies last two to three years and prepare pupils for occupations as skilled workers or service personnel—for instance, miners, electricians, sales assistants, waiters; (2) *secondary technical schools*, in which studies last four to five years and prepare pupils for work in middle-level technical, administrative, medical and educational posts; (3) *high schools*, in which studies last four years and comprise a general program preparing pupils for higher (college or university-type) education.

At the tertiary level there are two educational tracks: institutions of higher education and two-year post-secondary schools. Institutions of higher education with four- to seven-year programs differ with respect to the specializations offered to prospective students. The most important institutions are universities (law, social science, natural science, and others), polytechnics or technical universities (engineering specializations), medical academies, higher pedagogical institutes, agricultural institutes, economics institutes, and academies of fine art. Two-year post-secondary schools provide programs of vocational training.

The number of openings in particular branches of secondary and tertiary education is predetermined by either the Ministry of Education or the Ministry of Science, Higher Education, and Technology, depending on the kind of institution. Candidates for post-elementary education take part in competitive admission exams or go through other institutionalized channels of selection. Only those who completed high school or secondary technical school can compete for places leading to tertiary education. High-school graduates not accepted into a university-type institution can obtain vocational training in a two-year post-secondary school.

An important component of the Polish educational system are *schools for working people* (adult education for the employed), which offer courses parallel to those offered in the regular program for younger students.[1] Thus adults working full- or part-time have the opportunity to receive further education through courses offered in the evening or during non-working days. Diplomas and degrees from these schools are considered formally equivalent to those obtained in regular schools. Poland's educational system is almost entirely state-run and programs are uniform and centrally determined. Education at all levels is free.

Data

The data presented here were collected in a nationwide study of persons aged 25 to 44, conducted in 1981. A quota sample was arrived at based on the following control variables: sex, age (four categories), education (four levels), place of residence (town or country), and region (49 provinces). In selecting the sample a joint multivariate distribution of all control variables was used. A total of 1,526 individuals were finally interviewed.

Our research represents a "life-cycle" study, in that we collected information about the course of a person's educational, occupational, and migratory career as well as his or her family history. Particular emphasis was placed on obtaining detailed information about the respondent's educational career. In addition, respondents were asked to answer a series of questions about their perception of education as a factor affecting social differentiation; the question about educational prestige was one of several pertaining to the psychological aspects of educational inequality.

A method used in the studies of occupational prestige was adopted as a measurement of educational prestige, with descriptions of educational categories substituted for the occupational titles.[2] Respondents were asked to evaluate twenty educational categories differentiated in terms of: (1) level of schooling; (2) whether schooling at a particular level was completed or not; (3) whether education was obtained in the regular program or in a

Table 1

Distribution of Prestige for Twenty Categories of Schooling

Categories of schooling[a]	Percent of no response	Arithmetic mean[b]	Standard deviation[b]
Polytechnic institute, education completed	5.4	82.8	19.1
University, education completed	5.8	82.6	19.7
Medical school, education completed	5.1	81.6	20.8
Pedagogical institute, education completed	5.7	74.9	22.3
College with program for employed persons, education completed	4.4	74.4	22.0
Agricultural institute, education completed	4.3	74.3	20.9
Technical secondary school for employed persons, education completed	4.3	61.7	19.5
Two-year post-secondary school (college), education completed	5.0	61.5	17.6
Technical secondary school, education completed	5.3	58.9	16.3
High school for employed persons, education completed	4.9	57.0	20.3
High school, education completed	4.5	56.5	18.1
College, education not completed (two-year attendance)	4.8	55.3	20.4
Three-year post-elementary vocational school, education completed	4.8	45.4	19.4
Technical secondary school, education not completed (two year attendance)	4.8	41.3	19.7
Elementary school, education completed	4.4	39.9	23.9
High school, education not completed (two year attendance)	6.4	38.6	20.7
Elementary school with simplified program for employed persons, education completed	4.7	27.3	25.8
Three-year post elementary vocational school, education not completed (two year attendance)	6.0	26.3	22.6
Elementary school, education not completed (six grades)	6.0	25.9	24.7
Elementary school, education not completed (four grades)	4.8	19.5	24.9

[a]Categories of schooling are ordered according to average evaluation of prestige; in the questionnaire they were listed in random order.
[b]Numerical values for categories of schooling are: 100-very high; 75-high; 50-average; 25-low; 0-very low.

school for employed persons; (4) whether the school followed a normal or a simplified program; (5) the type of secondary school attended; (6) and the type of tertiary institution attended. Although we did not exhaust all possible combinations of criteria relevant to the Polish educational system, we did seek to include as many of the typical ones as possible. Table 1 shows all educational categories used in the analysis.

The prestige of particular categories of education was assessed by respondents on a five-point scale, ranging from very low to very high. We deliberately excluded the answer "difficult to say" from the multiple choice, available to respondents. Our objective was to compel respondents to express a decisive view on each of the educational categories presented to them. Interviewers were instructed to ask respondents their reasons for refusing to answer a question whenever "no response" occurred.

Results

We begin our analysis by looking at the cases of "no response." This residual category can be divided into two types. The first occurred when the respondent did not evaluate one or several educational categories but did assess others. Respondents who encountered difficulties in reaching an evaluation account for from .7 to 2.8 percent, depending on the educational category evaluated. The highest percentages correspond to the extreme categories—that is, four grades of elementary school or a university-type education. The second kind of "no response" occurred when a respondent refused to evaluate the categories presented to him. This took place in 3.1 percent of the cases. Most often respondents explained their refusal to answer by saying "people should not evaluate each other solely in terms of education."

These two kinds of "no response" are collapsed and shown in the last column of Table 1. In addition, 5.3 percent of respondents gave the same evaluation for all educational categories. In sum both "no response" and "indifferent" answers accounted for 8.4 percent of all cases. This proportion is no greater than that typically found in studies of occupational prestige. For the vast majority of individuals, differentiating prestige in terms of various educational categories did not present any difficulty.

The hierarchy of educational categories in terms of prestige is presented in Figure 1. It can easily be observed that the average evaluation for particular educational categories is broken down into four separate groupings, corresponding to the incomplete elementary, elementary, secondary, and tertiary levels of education. This division explains more than 95 percent of the entire variance of scores ($r = .988$). Thus, an important finding emerges: among the criteria considered by the respondents in their evaluation of specific educational categories, the dominant one is educational level.

This result is not surprising, given that formal education is received exclusively through participation in a hierarchical system in which particular levels correspond to the termination points of an educational career. In Poland's educational system three levels of schooling are clearly distinguishable—elementary, secondary, and tertiary. They are separated by barriers of institutionalized mechanisms of selection, such as admission exams, grades from earlier levels of schooling, and diplomas. In effect, transition from one level to another is much more important than interschool transfers at the same level. Typically, completion of an educational career corresponds to completion of a given educational level, and this is reflected in prestige ascribed by respondents to particular educational categories.

The difference in the evaluation of completed and uncompleted elementary education stems in part from history. Before World War II elementary schools in Poland were differentiated organizationally into full-term and reduced-term schools. The majority of young pupils, primarily in rural areas, attended reduced-term schools, which offered only a very limited program (four or six years). Completing education in these schools did not give students the right to apply to high school; the educational level of those who attended such schools has been officially classified (in

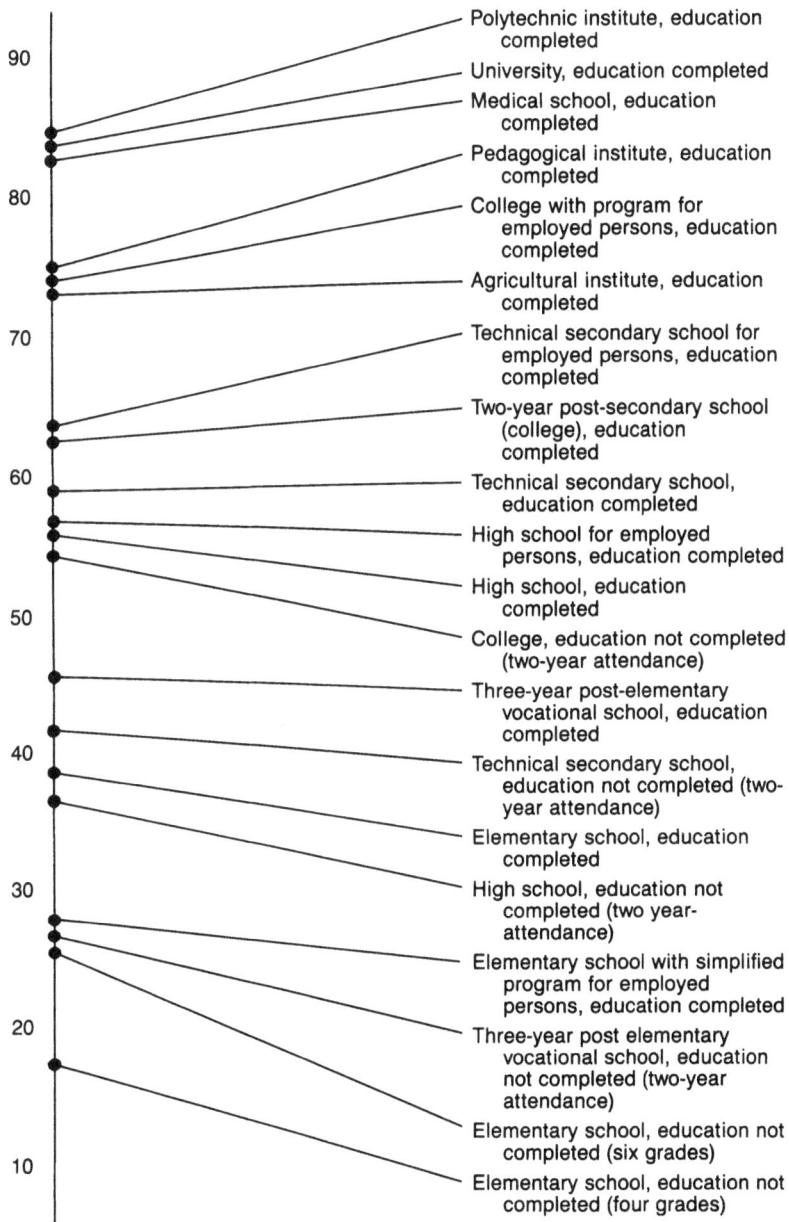

Figure 1. Average evaluation of prestige for educational categories.

Table 2

Correlations among Prestige Hierarchies of Occupation and Correlations among Prestige Hierarchies of Education for Groups of Persons with Different Sociodemographic Attributes

Group of persons	Prestige of education (Poland)	Prestige of occupations (Poland)[a]	Prestige of education (Poland)	Prestige of occupations (various countries)[c]
	Spearman's coefficient[b]		Pearson's coefficient[d]	
Men and women	.991	[e]	.998	.98–.99
Age groups	.985	.974	.995	[e]
Educational groups	.980	.946	.994	[e]
Town and country residents	.989	.948	.997	.86–.96
Income groups	.976	.967	.994	[e]
Occupational groups	.985	.975	.992	.96

[a]Source: Pohoski, Słomczyński and Wesołowski (1976: 64-66); the authors presented the values of Spearman's coefficients separately for various studies and this table includes the mean of these coefficients.

[b]In cases of divisions into more than two groups Spearman's coefficient is computed for the extreme groups.

[c]Source: Treiman (1977: 61-74).

[d]In cases of divisions into more than two groups Pearson's coefficient is computed for each pair of groups and the table gives the average value.

[e]Data unobtainable.

governmental statistics) as "incomplete elementary." In social consciousness the distinction between these types of elementary schooling persists, even though a uniform elementary school system was established after the war.

Since all the adults have direct experience with the school system, one would expect a high degree of consensus in the evaluation of educational prestige across social groups. It was hypothesized that intergroup consensus about educational prestige should be greater than intergroup consensus about occupational prestige. The simple justification for this hypothesis is that the system of occupational roles along a vertical dimension is not as transparent as the educational system.

Our data substantiate the hypothesis of greater intergroup consensus about educational prestige than about occupational prestige. Table 2 presents the values of correlation coefficients characterizing the similarity between evaluations of educational prestige obtained from groups distinguished in terms of sex, age, education, place of residence, income, and occupation. The congruence of evaluations is remarkable. The average value of Pearson's correlation of educational prestige score for each intergroup division exceeds 0.99. Where comparison is possible, we find that the correlations for educational prestige are higher than those for occupational prestige.

Students of social stratification often emphasize that the prestige of particular occupations is highly correlated with the skills required for such occupations. Skills constitute an important aspect of power and they affect income received. For these reasons skills indirectly influence the location of a given occupation in the hierarchy of prestige. This thesis is frequently corroborated in empirical studies in which education is adopted as an approximate indicator of skills. Treiman (1977: 114) estimates that in fifteen countries the average correlation between occupational prestige and the average education required for that occupation is .72. The correlation for Poland (.872) is even higher (Słomczyński and Kacprowicz, 1979: 99).

Discussion

To what degree can educational prestige be reduced to occupational prestige? Does it represent a certain distinctive dimension of stratification, or is it simply an aspect of a common dimension? On the basis of numerous studies of occupational prestige one can assume that educational prestige, reflecting educational levels, is strongly correlated with occupational prestige. It follows that educational prestige helps describe the common dimension of social stratification whose universal nature cross-nationally and diachronically was demonstrated by Treiman (1977). This does not mean, however, that educational prestige is completely reducible to occupational prestige. We examine these differences by returning to the hierarchy of prestige of educational categories listed in Figure 1.

Respondents evaluated incomplete education at every level in a specific way. "Two years of higher education" was on the average evaluated as being slightly lower than completed secondary education, even though the former required a longer period of study. We observe an analogous inconsistency with regard to the evaluation of uncompleted vocational school. The evaluation of this level of schooling is, on the average, 13.6 points lower than the evaluation of completed elementary school—a prerequisite for enrollment in a vocational school. Two grades of technical school and two grades of high school were evaluated as being lower than one would expect on the basis of years of schooling.

Our results demonstrate that respondents negatively evaluated the very fact of not finishing studies, regardless of the level. The interpretation of these results involves two characteristics of the Polish school system. First, schools at all levels are free and, accordingly, the economic situation (income) does not usually play a crucial role in interrupting a person's educational career. Second, the school system is strongly differentiated horizontally, so that a pupil may always opt for a school that corresponds to his ability. We can assume, therefore, that a person's not finishing school is commonly interpreted as a result of his or her not displaying sufficient industriousness, sense of responsibility, moral fiber, or "survival instincts." These qualities, necessary in obtaining an education, are more highly valued than education itself, as empirical research has documented (Wiśniewski, 1980). Accordingly, we believe that incomplete education, regardless of the level, is ascribed relatively low prestige because persons failing to complete a particular level of education are perceived as not possessing some universally valued attributes.

Other data also confirm this hypothesis. Completion of technical secondary education designed for working people is evaluated as being significantly higher than finishing the corresponding type of school in the regular program. The majority of students attending technical secondary schools for adults are people who ventured onto the labor market immediately after finishing elementary or vocational school and resumed schooling several years later while continuing to work. In social consciousness persons who obtain such an education show ambition, concern for improving their knowledge and skills, and the desire to advance both socially and occupationally.

The evaluation of tertiary education will be examined in some detail. Average evaluations are clearly divided into two groups depending on the type of tertiary education obtained. Polytechnics, universities, and medical academies are evaluated highly, while agricultural and pedagogical institutes and institutions with programs for working people (without specification of the type of institution) have relatively low evaluations (Figure 1). Initially we assumed that this difference could be interpreted as resulting from the difference in the prestige of *occupational* positions which graduates of the respective institutions go on to fill. To test this hypothesis the following analysis was carried out. Using the Polish standard scale of prestige[3] we ascribed values of prestige to about 100 selected occupational categories. For each occupational category we listed the type of tertiary educational institution that was most commonly completed by the individuals in a given occupation. This enabled us to calculate the scores of occupational prestige of the graduates from each of the institutions under consideration. Comparison of these scores does not fully corroborate the initial hypothesis. In particular, graduates of agricultural institutes enjoy the same occupational prestige as do graduates of polytechnics, universities, and medical schools. Education at pedagogical institutes leads to occupations with clearly lower prestige than does education at agricultural institutes, even though both are classified, according to educational prestige, in the same group (cf. Figure 1).

The prestige of an occupation that can be pursued upon graduating from a given institution of tertiary education is not a decisive criterion, and in any case certainly not the only one affecting educational prestige. The best empirically validated hypothesis explaining differences in the prestige of various institutions is the following: institutions transmitting the culture of higher social strata are evaluated as being higher than others in terms of prestige. In particular, the values of the intelligentsia include broad knowledge, a refined taste for cultural goods, erudition, wisdom, sound judgment, courtesy, and tolerance. The social makeup of students indicates that tertiary educational institutions can be differentiated in terms of transmitting the values of the intelligentsia. In polytechnics, universities, and medical schools the majority of students are from the intelligentsia stratum; in institutions given lower evaluations (agricultural and pedagogical institutes, higher-educational institutions with programs for working people), the majority of students are of working-class or peasant origin. Even if the two groups of institutions were not differentiated in terms of the intentional transmission of intelligentsia values, the influence of the students' social origins could bring about differences as a consequence of the internalization and intergenerational transmission of these values.

Our study shows that people regard values corresponding to the culture of higher social strata as an important component of education. The evidence is in the answers to a question posed in our study: "Who do you consider to be an educated person?" Apart from formal education, respondents also identified a series of other attributes that in their opinion should be displayed by an educated person. Qualities characteristic of the culture of higher social strata were mentioned about twice as often as those related to occupational skills—knowledge required for pursuing a profession, the congruence of skills obtained with the occupation pursued, or the ability to apply acquired knowledge to practical situations.

The hypothesis that institutions that largely transmit intelligentsia values are ranked highly does not extend to the secondary-school level. Here the technical school is more highly esteemed than the high school, although the former places greater stress on occupationally relevant rather than general forms of knowledge. Moreover, pupils of working-class or peasant background clearly constitute a larger proportion in technical schools than in high schools. Some explanation for the respondents' higher evaluation of technical rather than high schools is provided by analyzing answers to the question on "an educated person." Among the respondents who indicated secondary-level education as sufficient to consider someone "an educated person," technical education was about three times more frequently mentioned than general high-school education. Respondents prefer to associate the secondary-education level with the attainment of occupational skills rather than with internalization of the values of the intelligentsia. At the tertiary level the order of preference is reversed.

Conclusions

The data presented show that educational prestige can be as successfully studied as occupational prestige, employing an analogous empirical method. The obtained hierarchy of educational categories is, in its broad outline, consistent with the hierarchy of occupational prestige. This strongly suggests that both educational and occupational prestige are dual aspects of a common, more general dimension of stratification.

Respondents' evaluations indicate specific features of the hierarchy of educational prestige as compared to that of occupational prestige. The evaluations of educational categories are influenced by such characteristics of the Polish educational system as high interlevel attrition and low intensity of movement between schools of the same level. The results also suggest that certain elements of the Polish system of values strongly affect the evaluation of educational prestige. In particular, the higher evaluation given to education obtained at polytechnics, universities, and medical schools than to education obtained at pedagogical or agricultural institutes is consistent with certain values of the intelligentsia.

The similarity of the hierarchies of educational prestige among the groups of respondents with different characteristics of social position is stronger than in the case of occupational prestige (cf. Table 2). This result can be explained by the ease of perceiving the mechanisms determining the functioning of the educational system.

Notes

1. In 1978, for 100 graduates from each level and type of school for youth (regular program) there were the following numbers of graduates from corresponding schools for working people (adult education): secondary technical schools—79; high school—30; two-year post-secondary schools—42; schools of higher education—80 (*Główny Urząd Statystyczny*, 1979).

2. The question read: "We would like to find out how people in our country evaluate persons with differing levels and types of education. Below you will find a list of up to 20 individuals having various kinds of education. Please evaluate these individuals in terms of the recognition and respect you have for them, focusing exclusively on the education they possess. Please reach an evaluation even if you believe people should not judge each other in terms of education alone."

3. The Polish standard scale of prestige was developed by Słomczyński and Kacprowicz (1979).

References

Blaikie, N. W. H.
    1977   "The meaning and measurement of occupational prestige."
              Australian and New Zealand Journal of Sociology 13: 102–115

Główny Urząd Statystyczny [Central Statistical Office]
    1979   *Rocznik Statystyczny Szkolnictwa 1978/79*. [Yearbook of Educational Statistics 1978/79.] Warsaw: Central Statistical Office

Goldthorpe, J. H., and K. Hope
    1974   *The Social Grading of Occupations: A New Approach and Scale*. Oxford: Clarendon Press.

Pohoski, M., K. M. Słomczyński and W. Wesołowski
    1976   "Occupational prestige in Poland, 1958–1975." *Polish Sociological Bulletin* 4(36): 63–77.

Sarapata, A.
    1975   "Z badań nad hierarchią prestiżu zajęć w Polsce." [Research on the hierarchy of occupational prestige in Poland.] *Studia Socjologiczne* 1(56): 47–67.

Sarapata, A. and W. Wesołowski
    1961   "The evaluation of occupations by Warsaw inhabitants." *American Journal of Sociology* 66: 581–591.

Słomczyński, K. M., and G. Kacprowicz

1979 *Skale Zawodów*. [Scales of Occupations.] Warsaw: Institute of Philosophy and Sociology of the Polish Academy of Sciences.
Treiman, D. J.
    1977 *Occupational Prestige in Comparative Perspective*. New York: Academic Press.
Wesołowski, W., and K. M. Słomczyński
    1977 *Investigations on Class Structure and Social Stratification in Poland, 1945-1975*. Warsaw: Institute of Philosophy and Sociology of the Polish Acdemy of Sciences.
Wiśniewski, W.
    1980 "Education as a value in Polish society." *International Journal of Political Education* 3: 239-253.

Value Systems among Occupational Groups

MARIA MISZTAL

This paper is concerned with the value systems of various occupational categories; the systems are identified by applying the rule of generating preferential group ranking and by analysis of individual cases. Our study shows that value systems are differentiated depending on occupational category. Differences in the professed value systems are related to two aspects of social differentiation: type of work and socioeconomic status. Such differences involve both the rank order in which values appear and the type of relationships among them.

Our analysis is based on data from a questionnaire survey administered to a nationwide sample in 1977. A total of 5,594 persons, ranging in age from 15 to 45, were included in the quota sample. The representativeness of the sample was controlled in terms of the distribution of such factors as sex, age, place of residence, and education. All generalizations of results for men and women between 15 and 45 years of age are given without determination of the size of the sampling error.

This research is part of a broader project, "Value systems and consumption patterns in Polish society," sponsored by the Ministry of Science, Higher Education, and Technology and the Polish Academy of Sciences; the project was coordinated by Professor Jerzy J. Wiatr. Research was conducted by the Sociological Research Group on Education, directed by Professor W. Wiśniewski, at the University of Warsaw. This paper is based on Misztal (1982).

Theoretical assumptions

The approach adopted is based on the assumption that values constitute an element of social consciousness. In defining values we can refer to Kluckhohn's (1962) understanding that values are "a conception of what I ought to want." In addition, it is assumed that the specific components of consciousness called "values" are characterized by the simultaneous appearance of cognitive, emotional, and normative dimensions. Apart from knowledge, and emotional and normative orientations, a constituent element of values is the conviction that a given thing, state of affairs, or way of acting is an appropriate and socially acceptable object of human desire and striving. Values are the basis of human actions and, more precisely, the criteria governing choices.

We also introduce the concepts of value system and structure of a value system. By "value system" we mean a collection of values having a particular type of linkage. The relationship among values forming part of a given system connotes the structure of this system. In this context the relationships of preference and indifference will be considered.

The concept of value system includes numerous sets of values difficult to account for in a single sociological research project. In the present study we focus on four values: happy family life, educational achievement, high income, and altruistic social action. People are constantly compelled to make choices among these values in their daily lives.

The values selected were assumed to be homogeneous and were compared by the survey respondents. In designing the survey questions an attempt was made to eliminate noncomparable values which, in Ossowski's (1967) terminology, constitute a disharmonious scale of values. Such a scale would apply particularly to values Ossowski described as "ceremonial," in contrast to those examined here, which are "quotidian" in nature.

Our concern with comparability explains the exclusion of such values as "justice," "equality," or "liberty." These undoubtedly would be of interest to respondents, but they seemed noncomparable with such values as "happy family life" or "educational achievement." Moreover, during the period in which the research was conducted, the excluded values did not form part of a coherent system of values; they were largely "ceremonial" in nature and influenced choices made by Poles only to a limited degree. However, the political events that took place in Poland in 1980–81 changed this situation: for a large proportion of the population the values of justice, equality, and liberty became the basis for many choices. During that period these values could have conflicted with the ones we investigate in this paper.

According to Ossowski (1967), some ceremonial values are professed in periods when social bonds are particularly intense; the years 1980–81 were precisely such a time. Ceremonial values came to approximate quotidian ones and the two types may actually have fused into one coherent system.[1]

Method of data collection

The basis for our analysis is the series of respondents' answers to a question about paired values that were juxtaposed. An introductory part of the survey question read: "People set for themselves various goals in life that they consider important. However, it often happens that people must choose among goals. Below we present several goals listed in pairs. We are interested in knowing whether you believe that one should strive toward them simultaneously or whether occasionally one has to give up on one goal in order to attain the other. Please indicate your choice in each of the cases listed."

As essential part of the question read: "In this fast-paced era when time is always lacking, a person should above all strive for . . ." Four values were then presented in pairs, with each combination given, totaling six sets of alternatives. The four values were: (1) a happy family life; (2) educational achievement; (3) high income; and (4) altruistic social action. The respondent was required to give one of two answers: either selecting a particular value from each set or asserting that both values were equally important.

Method of data analysis

The analysis of value systems was undertaken at both group and individual levels. The first level is analyzed by using two rules for generating preferential group rankings: Borda's rule and the optimal prediction rule.[2] Preferential group ranking, assigned to a collectivity, is supposed to represent the choices of its individual members most accurately. In this analysis we refer to preferential group rankings as representing group value systems.

The basis for determining group value systems is the analysis of paired choices of values. The distribution of respondents choosing one value over another or treating both values as equally important is presented in Table 1. We use the following notation: $i > j$ denotes that value i is preferred to value j, and $i \approx j$ denotes indifference between values i and j.

Borda's rule for determining group value systems consists of computing the number of cases in which a given value is preferred over any other value, and the number of cases in which any other value is preferred over the given one. Differences in these magnitudes, ranked in decreasing order, yield the final result—that is, the group value system. The group system of four values, established on the basis of this procedure, yields the following form: $1 > 2 > 3 > 4$. Table 1 shows that the most esteemed value is a happy family life; it is followed by educational achievement; the next place in the hierarchy is taken by attaining high income, and after that comes altruistic social action.

The data analyzed using Borda's rule concern only clear-cut choices made by the respondents; indifference between values is excluded from analysis. When the rule of optimal prediction is applied, all possible patterns of value choices are considered. The rule of optimal prediction leads to the selection of a group value system that best predicts the value systems of all individuals. This rule generates a ranking of values that minimizes the assumed loss

Table 1

Distribution of Preferential Rankings for All Pairs of Values[a]

Values[b]		i>j	i≈j	j>i
i	j			
1	2	1,705	2,624	587
3	4	2,340	1,177	1,399
1	3	2,698	1,897	321
2	3	2,249	1,657	1,010
4	2	879	1,659	2,378
1	4	2,887	1,759	270

[a]The table excludes those who did not indicate their value preference in at least one pair of values. There were 678 respondents in this category.
[b]The identification numbers of values are: 1—happy family life; 2—educational achievement; 3—high income; 4—altruistic social action.

function. In prediction, each individual ranking of values is compared to a hypothetical group ranking of values; the loss is a real number n which represents the estimate of prediction error. When the rule of optimal prediction is applied, we assume that: (1) the loss function is not negative; (2) if the prediction is accurate, the prediction loss is 0; and (3) the loss function is monotonic with respect to prediction error. Table 2 presents the matrix describing the loss function.

In the construction of group value systems the loss related to prediction error, which involves predicting a "strong" preference (e.g., A over B) while individual preference is the opposite (e.g., B over A), is assumed to be 2. The loss related to predicting a "strong" preference while individual preference ranking gives equal weight to both values, or the converse situation, is assumed to be 1. Correct prediction is scored 0. Accordingly, the loss function applied in the construction of group value systems takes the following form.[3]

$$L = \begin{matrix} 0 & 1 & 2 \\ 1 & 0 & 1 \\ 2 & 1 & 0 \end{matrix}$$

Table 2

Matrix of the Loss Function

Relations of individual preferences between pairs of values	Relations of group preferences between pairs of values		
	i>j	i≈j	j>i
i>j	n_{11}	n_{12}	n_{13}
i≈j	n_{21}	n_{22}	n_{23}
j>i	n_{31}	n_{32}	n_{33}

Application of the rule of optimal prediction is based on the matrix of distribution of value choices. The procedure consists of multiplying the matrix of the loss function (n); the obtained matrix contains the sum of the losses related to the prediction of individual choices for each particular pair of values on the basis of the respective group choices. The optimal choice is, then, selected from each row of the matrix, that is, for each pair of values; it represents preferential group ranking for which the sum of losses is minimal. If the selected choices between values are transitive, we then obtain the ranking of values for each category of respondents. If the relations are not transitive, a different computational technique must be adopted.[4]

The application of the optimal prediction rule to the data on all respondents yielded a two-part value system: $1 \approx 2 < 3 \approx 4$. First place in the system is taken by the values of happy family life and educational achievement, each being equally important. Second place is occupied by high income and altruistic social action, which are also treated as equally important.

Our analysis is complemented by an examination of the four values at the individual level. Using a similar method to score answers, we fit each respondent to a given value system.[5] In the next section we describe the value systems of particular occupational categories and present the modal value systems, determined on the individual level.

Table 3

Group and Individual Systems of Four Values According to Socio-occupational Category[a]

Occupational category	No. of respondents	Value systems[b] according to		
		Borda's rule	Optimal prediction rule	Modal ordering
Professionals in nontechnical fields	164	1>2>4>3	1≈2>3≈4	1≈2≈4>3
Professionals in technical fields	173	1>2>4>3	1≈2≈3≈4	1≈2≈4≈3
				1>2>4>3
Managers	48	1>2>3>4	1≈2>3≈4	1≈2≈3≈4
Technicians	338	1>2>3>4	1≈2>3≈4	1≈2≈4>3
Office workers	439	1>2>3>4	1≈2>3≈4	1>2>3>4
Service workers	292	1>2>3>4	1>2≈3≈4	1>2>3>4
Entrepreneurs	74	1>2>3>4	1>2≈3≈4	1≈2>3>4
Foremen	218	1>2>3>4	1≈2≈3>4	1≈2≈3>4
Skilled manual workers	1,029	1>2>3>4	1≈2≈3>4	1>3>2>4
Semi-skilled manual workers	325	1>2>3>4	1≈2≈3>4	1>3>2>4
Unskilled workers	209	1>2>3>4	1≈2≈3>4	1≈2≈3>4
Private farmers	514	1>2>3>4	1≈2≈3>4	1>3>2>4
Family members helping on private farms	221	1>2>3>4	1≈2≈3>4	1≈2≈3>4
Agricultural laborers	97	1>2>3>4	1≈2≈3>4	1≈2≈3>4
Students	1,029	1>2>4>3	1≈2>3≈4	1≈2≈4>3
Persons neither working nor studying	381	1>2>3>4	1≈2≈3>4	1>3>2>4

[a]The division into occupational categories was carried out according to the classification developed by Pohoski, Słomczyński and Milczarek (1974); see also: Pohoski and Słomczyński (1978).

[b]The identification numbers of values are: 1—happy family life; 2—educational achievement; 3—high income; 4—altruistic social action.

Value systems of occupational categories

Table 3 presents the results for fourteen occupational categories and two additional groups of respondents: those who were neither working nor studying, and those who were students. The application of Borda's rule differentiates to only a small degree the value systems professed by members of various occupational categories. Three categories profess a value system different from the one held by all other groups of respondents; these categories are: professionals in nontechnical fields, professionals in technical fields, and students. Like other groups, they value happy family life most highly, and then educational achievement. Third place in the hierarchy is given to altruistic social action, which, in these groups, took precedence over high income aspirations.

The group value system that corresponds to occupational categories becomes highly differentiated when the optimal prediction rule is applied. The ranking of the four values that most accurately characterizes the entire sample turns out to be the one typical for professionals in nontechnical fields, managers, technicians, nonmanual workers, and students. The value system held by professionals in technical fields is not hierarchical since no two values are linked to each other in a preferential relationship. The value systems of service workers and entrepreneurs are distinguished by the highest rank of happy fmaily life, which is shared by no other value, as it is in other occupational categories. Educational achievement is regarded as a value equal in importance to high income and altruistic social action. Foremen, manual workers of varying skills, and farmers prefer a value system in which three values are considered equally important and share first place: happy family life, educational achievement, and high income.

When the optimal prediction rule is used, the major line of division in the profession of values seems to be that delineated by the nature of work performed. White-collar-type work is associated with lower importance accorded to high income. In contrast, manual-type work is linked to greater emphasis on high income and less on altruistic social action. These regularities, however, do not pertain to the category of professionals in technical fields.

Value systems established at the individual level appear to be more differentiated than those at the group level. If we begin our analysis with the first four occupational categories in Table 3, we observe that altruistic social action was valued more than, or at least equally with, high income; for categories from entrepreneurs to students, high income precedes altruistic social action, but the remaining values are esteemed less than educational achievement. Generally, if we treat the occupational categories listed in Table 3 as a social hierarchy, we can then state that the transition from higher to lower categories is accompanied by an increase in the importance of high income and a decline in the importance of educational achievement and altruistic social action.

The analysis of modal value systems established links between, on the one hand, findings about the place of altruistic social action and income in the value system according to Borda's rule and, on the other, findings about the place of income in the value system according to the optimal prediction rule.

Interpretation of findings

The differences in results are at least to some extent a function of the statistical procedures applied and the broad range of information contained in the empirical data the procedures take into consideration. An important methodological implication emerging from the analysis is that a value system need not always take the form of a hierarchy. This is substantiated by the result obtained for professionals in technical fields by applying the optimal prediction rule and also by analyzing cases at the individual level. Specialists in technical fields treat all four values as equally important, and the hierarchical structure collapses to one point. This finding should serve as a warning to sociological investigators who construct hierarchies of values. For at least some social groups such a construction may turn out to be artifactual.

When some values are treated as equally important, this indifference may be regarded as an indication that the value system under consideration has a complex structure. It may show the difficulty a respondent encounters in comparing these values, and therefore be an indication of their incommensurable nature. In appropriately designed research on values, comparability or noncomparability can be determined directly by respondents. Further research into the complex structure of value systems should probe more deeply into the nature of the evaluation process.

The differentiation of value systems was shown to be related to two aspects of social differentiation: the nature of work and socioeconomic status. Educational achievement and altruistic social action are values more highly esteemed by individuals performing nonmanual work; they consider income less important. By contrast, persons working in manual jobs tend to rank income above educational achievement and altruistic social action. The significance of the latter two values is greater the higher the socioeconomic status of the category to which the respondent belongs. A high socioeconomic status is inversely related to the importance of income as a value.

The obtained results can be interpreted in terms of the varying degree to which the needs of respondents are satisfied. In line with Maslow's theory of needs, we expect that failure to satisfy needs relating to want implies that the corresponding values have gained a prominent place in the system.[6] In our study these involve needs related to income as a value. In contrast, improved satisfaction of needs relating to want is associated with a lower position for the values corresponding to them in the hierarchy. This also implies greater importance of the values that correspond to the needs relating to growth, identified in this study with educational achievement and altruistic social action.

Another explanation can be be offered for the lower place given income and the higher place altruistic social action has in the value systems of persons who enjoy high socioeconomic status and are engaged in nonmanual work. They are concerned less with the objective situation than with the traditional value system of the intelligentsia in Poland. Their value system and personality models emphasized attitudes of social activism and the deprecation of money as a major value and goal in life.[7] The transmission of such an orientation to the younger generation can take place within the intelligentsia family when individuals inherit their parents' socioeconomic status. It can also occur in school, with exposure to late nineteenth- and early twentieth-century Polish literature. The traditional values of the intelligentsia are consistent with values that constitute an element of socialist ideology, and they are inculcated into young people at school.[8]

The hypothesis that the traditional values of the intelligentsia influence value systems in Poland today appears to receive specific substantiation for professionals in nontechnical and technical fields. The former above all continue the traditional careers of the Polish intelligentsia, that is, careers oriented in a humanistic rather than a technical direction. In addition, professionals in nontechnical fields are exposed in a more intense and protracted way to adult socialization influences during their careers. They work under occupational conditions that generally offer less income and fewer opportunities to earn additional income, but spare them from constant concern about economic conditions.

In the case of professionals in technical fields, less intense exposure to the traditional value system of the Polish intelligentsia can be assumed. Moreover, a larger proportion of professionals in technical fields have origins in the working class and peasantry than is the case for professionals in nontechnical fields. Thus, the system of four values characteristic of technical professionals represents a compromise between traditional intelligentsia values inculcated in youth and values promoted by a sociooccupational situation that distinguishes these persons from other sections of the intelligentsia. In addition, technical professionals, accustomed to a precise way of thinking, may have encountered greater difficulty comparing values they considered noncomparable. Accordingly, technical professionals choose responses that assign equal weight to the values in a particular pair more frequently than do other respondents.

The value systems in which a prominent position is occupied by altruistic social action seem to be functional from the standpoint of some types of occupational career. Striving for this value may be linked with skill in interpersonal contacts, or with the relationship between advancement into "higher" occupational categories and organizational membership. Such linkages seem to be stronger for nontechnical than for technical professionals, since for the former "human relations" criteria of on-the-job activity are used, while for the latter the criteria refer to productivity.

When greater importance is assigned to educational achievement, the significance of income as a value generally diminishes. In the social consciousness educational achievement is associated with economic cost. Persons not wishing or unable to absorb such costs do not in fact adopt a value system that denigrates the importance of income. The elevated place of income in a hierarchy of values encourages the termination of education at lower levels of formal schooling and, as a result, leads to the attainment of occupational positions having lower socioeconomic status and prestige.

These concluding remarks suggest that values play an active part in the process of attaining occupational position. It is theoretically possible that professed values influence an occupational career and, in turn, that values are shaped by occupational position and the nature of work performed.[9]

Notes

1. Nowak (1981) has drawn attention to the utility of studying values of a "ceremonial" nature even in periods when they do not directly affect human actions.
2. Borda's rule is presented in de Grazia (1953). An axiomatic treatment of this rule is given by Young (1974). The rule of optimal prediction was formulated by Lissowski (1974).
3. Derivation of the loss function is based on the distance function between preferential rankings, axiomatically described by Kemeny (1962).
4. Using this procedure we choose from among all possible preferential rankings of values one that minimizes the loss function. The sum of losses is calculated by adding up the losses related to selected preferential rankings for each pair of values. Nontransitive preferential group ranking occurred when

the optimal prediction rule was applied to construct the value system of all respondents. We used some additional assumptions for application of the procedure; see Lissowski (1980).

5. Scoring the answers was carried out in the following way: 2 for a value that was selected as the more important in a pair; 1 for values treated as equally important; and 0 for the value deemed the less important in a pair. The maximum score that a given value could obtain was 6 and the minimum 0. The system of four values for each individual was reconstructed according to the decreasing score obtained by particular values.

6. Maslow (1959; 1962). A similar interpretation of Maslow's theory of needs was the basis for the cross-cultural comparative research of Inglehart (1977). Some of his results seem consistent with those presented in this paper.

7. Some analyses point up the hypocritical attitude of the Polish intelligentsia toward economic goods. While the members of the intelligentsia have enjoyed relative affluence and considered this a natural state of affairs, they regard questions about their standard of living as embarrassing. See: Jawłowska and Mokrzycki (1978).

8. Jasińska and Siemieńska (1975).

9. This reciprocal causal relationship was identified by Misztal (1982). The study includes an analysis of the role of values and attitudes in the process of inheriting education and occupational status.

References

de Grazia, A.
    1953   "Mathematical derivation of an election system." *Isis* 44:42–51.

Inglehart, R.
    1977   *The Silent Revolution: Changing Values and Political Styles among Western Publics.* Princeton, N.J.: Princeton University Press.

Jasińska, A. and R. Siemieńska
    1975   *Wzory osobowe socjalizmu.* [Models of Socialist Personality.] Warsaw: Wiedza Powszechna.

Jawłowska, A. and E. Mokrzycki
    1978   "Style życia a przemiany struktury społecznej: propozycja typologii historyczno-socjologicznej." [Styles of life and transformations of social structure: a proposal for a historical-sociological typology.] Pp. 14–176 in A. Siciński (ed.), *Styl życia: przemiany we współczesnej Polsce.* [Style of Life: Transformations in Contemporary Poland.] Warsaw.

Kemeny, J.
    1962   "Preference rankings—an axiomatic approach." Pp. 9–23 in J. Kemeny and J. L. Snell (eds.), *Mathematical Models in the Social Sciences.* Boston: Blaisdel.

Kluckhohn, C.
  1962   "Values and value-orinetations in the theory of action: an exploration in definition and classification." Pp. 383–433 in T. Parsons and E. A. Shils (eds.), *Toward a General Theory of Action*. New York.
Lissowski, G.
  1974   "Statystyczny opis zbioru uporządkowań preferencyjnych." [A statistical description of the set of preference orderings.] *Prakseologia* 51-2 (No. 3-4): 379–413.
  1980   Sposoby wyznaczania grupowego uporządkowania preferencyjnego według reguły optymalnej predykcji. [Methods of Determination of Group Preference Ordering by Means of the Rule of Optimal Prediction.] Unpublished monograph.
Maslow, A. H.
  1959   "Psychological data and value theory." Pp. 119–36 in A. H. Maslow (ed.), *New Knowledge in Human Values*. New York.
  1962   *Toward a Psychology of Being*. New York.
Misztal, M.
  1982   *Zróżnicowanie systemów wartości społeczeństwa polskiego*. [Differentiation in the System of Values of Polish Society.] Warsaw: Polish Scientific Publishers.
Nowak, S.
  1981   "Values and attitudes of the Polish people." *Scientific American* 245 (July):45–53.
Ossowski, S.
  1967   "Konflikty niewspółmiernych skal wartości." [Conflicts of incommensurable scales of values.] In: *Z zagadnień psychologii społecznej. Dzieła* [Problems of Social Psychology. Works, vol. 3.] Warsaw: Polish Scientific Publishers.
Pohoski, M. and K. M. Słomczyński
  1978   *Społeczna klasyfikacja zawodów*. [Social Classification of Occupations.] Warsaw: Institute of Philosophy and Sociology of the Polish Academy of Sciences.
Pohoski, M., K. M. Słomczyński, and K. Milczarek
  1974   *Społeczna klasyfikacja zawodów*. [Social Classification of Occupations.] Warsaw: Institute of Philosophy and Sociology of the Polish Academy of Sciences.
Young, H. P.
  1974   "An axiomization of Borda's rule." *Journal of Economic Theory* 9:43–52.

Social Mobility

Actual, Perceived, and Equitable

TADEUSZ K. KRAUZE and
KAZIMIERZ M. SŁOMCZYŃSKI

Introduction

In sociology, intergenerational social mobility is usually studied in its "material" dimension, that is, as an objectively existing social process. Irrespective of the population considered and method of data collection, mobility is conceived in terms of the transitions of persons between their categories of origin and destination. Empirical analysis of social mobility begins with investigating the frequency of such transitions.

Parallel subjective dimensions involve images and preferences concerning the frequency of mobility in the social consciousness. Thus, one can ask: What are the perceived amounts of mobility between specific origins and destinations? What amounts of mobility are equitable? We pose these questions since social mobility, as a process experienced directly or indirectly by all members of a society, is an object of everyday evaluations and judgments (e.g. Janicka, 1976: 152-185; Goldthorpe, 1980:217-50; Harrop, 1980; Nowak, 1969; Narojek, 1982)

In this paper we attempt to compare three dimensions of mobility: "material" (corresponding to mobility that is objectively observable and verifiable), "cognitive" (corresponding to mo-

---

The authors are indebted to Wojciech Zaborowski and Bogdan W. Mach, who participated in the conceptualization of the research project. Dr. Zaborowski also supervised data collection and provided the initial tabulations needed for this paper.

bility perceived and expressed through popular beliefs), and "normative" (corresponding to mobility postulated according to group standards of equity). In comparing these dimensions we are interested in the differences between their *mobility regimes*. A mobility regime comprises the internal relationships among all mobility frequencies, invariant with respect to changes in the origin and destination distributions. Our research questions are:

1) To what extent is the actual mobility regime distorted in social consciousness?

2) To what extent is the equitable mobility regime different from the perceived one?

3) To what extent does the actual mobility regime depart from the equitable one?

In the theoretical part of this paper we show that answers to these questions are interpretable in terms of "popular perception," "justice evaluation," and "folk-norm legitimacy." By performing appropriate algebraic operations on the matrices of actual, perceived, and equitable mobility, we formalize some aspects of these concepts to measure the degree of false consciousness, the degree of the feeling of injustice, and the degree of illegitimacy in the domain of social mobility.

In the empirical part of the paper we rely on previously collected data on the actual frequencies of mobility transitions among major segments of Polish society. The data on perceived and equitable amounts of mobility among the same segments of society were elicited from a limited sample of university students. We describe in detail the procedure used in gathering data on both subjective types of mobility and a method of constructing the respective mobility tables for each individual. However, our analyses utilize these tables with frequencies averaged for the total sample of respondents to reflect modal perceptions and modal judgments. After presenting the matrices of actual, perceived, and equitable mobility we compare them with respect to their mobility regimes.

Problematics and formalization of concepts

Traditionally, research on social inequality maintains a balanced interest in the objective, cognitive, and normative dimensions, as is evident in the works of Marx and Weber. By contrast, recent research on social mobility is so heavily slanted toward studying the objective dimension of mobility that its cognitive and normative dimensions have not been elaborated in reviews of the literature (Kerckhoff, 1984; Matras, 1980; Simkus, 1981; Featherman, 1981; Mach et al., 1978; Mayer, 1979).

In this paper we attempt to integrate the objective, cognitive and normative dimensions of mobility in a unified framework by analyzing the relations between them (cf. Figure 1). The material dimension characterizes "what objectively exists": reality is described by means of frequencies of transitions among all origin and destination categories. Although these frequencies are not directly observed by members of society, we assume that rough estimates of the frequencies of mobility transitions are implied in people's images of the mobility process and, as such, are retrievable for assessment of "what is believed to be." By perceived mobility we mean a complete set of frequencies of mobility transitions inferred from people's beliefs about the distribution of members of each major segment of society according to social origin. The relation of "what is believed to be" to "what objectively exists" characterizes the popular perception of reality, and links the cognitive and material dimensions of social mobility. An inaccurate perception of reality corresponds to various degrees of "false consciousness" in the domain of social mobility.

Perceived mobility involves, at least indirectly, the class positions of evaluators and their class interests (Harrop, 1980); however, the term "false consciousness," referring to social mobility, is only vaguely reminiscent of its Marxian origin. Our usage is closer to "false social consciousness" than to "false class consciousness." In this paper we compare perceived mobility to actual mobility and account for distortions in perception independently of their class-related causes.

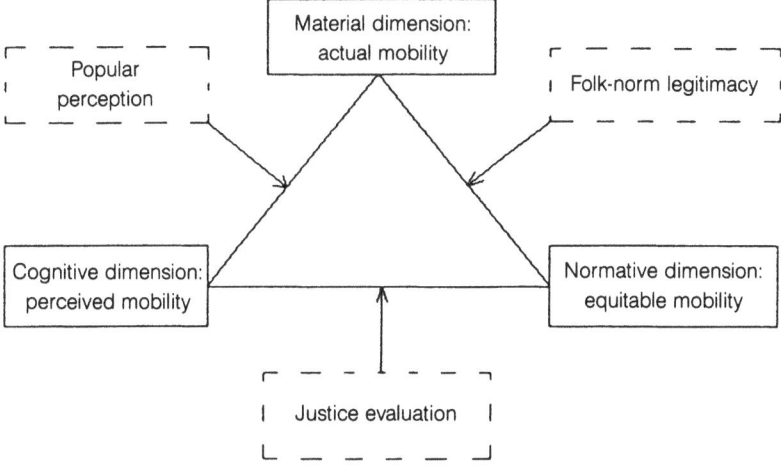

Figure 1. Material, cognitive, and normative dimensions of social mobility and relations resulting from their pairwise comparisons.

Equitable mobility is defined as the complete set of frequencies of mobility transitions that are inferred from people's judgements about the just distribution of destinations among persons originating in each of the major segments of society. Thus, equitable mobility frequencies are those that "ought to be" if group standards of justice are fulfilled. Since actual mobility is not directly observable by the members of a society, their "justice evaluation" involves a comparison of "what is believed to be" with "what ought to be." This evaluation, relating the normative and cognitive dimensions of social mobility, results in varying degrees of the feeling of injustice.

Actual mobility is rather strongly supported by the standards of equity or justice expressed through "folk norms." Thus, "what objectively exists" can be legitimized by "what ought to be," even though the relevant reality is misperceived or unknown. In the domain of social mobility, the relation of the material and normative dimensions reflects the essence of legitimacy. Mutatis mutandis, "legitimation is treated as a process in which the structure of the larger society becomes incorporated within the inner consciousness of the individual" (Della Fave, 1980:956). On the basis of the discrepancy between actual and equitable mobility, one can appraise the degree of illegitimacy of the objectively existing mobility.

The measures of false consciousness, feeling of injustice, and illegitimacy are provided in terms of operations on mobility matrices. Let us assume that we have empirically determined three matrices of social mobility, $A = (a_{ij})$, $P = (p_{ij})$, and $E = (e_{ij})$, containing frequencies of transitions from origin categories i to destination categories j. The entries of matrix A are observed frequencies, which describe the objective situation. The entries of matrices P and E are the perceived and equitable frequencies, respectively; they are considered to reflect the state of social consciousness attributed to a particular population.

We assume that all elements of matrices A, P, and E are positive. Under this assumption, the relations of P to A, E to P, and A to P are investigated. In each pair the first matrix is compared to the second matrix, which is treated as a standard. Comparisons are made in terms of ratios of corresponding elements of the mobility matrices. We express these ratios in the form of matrices $F = (f_{ij})$, $S = (s_{ij})$, and $L = (l_{ij})$, with elements defined as follows:

$$f_{ij} = p_{ij}/a_{ij} \quad s_{ij} = e_{ij}/p_{ij} \quad l_{ij} = a_{ij}/e_{ij} \quad \text{for all } i, j.$$

Matrices F, S, and L characterize the degrees, respectively, of false consciousness, feeling of injustice, and illegitimacy. Figure 2 shows the directions of comparisons among the pairs of matrices of actual, perceived, and equitable mobility as well as the algebraic operations used for these comparisons. The properties and implications of the proposed formalization will be discussed in some detail.

The values of ratios f_{ij}, s_{ij}, and l_{ij} range over all positive numbers. The value 1 means that no deviation exists between the value compared (the numerator) to its standard (the denomina-

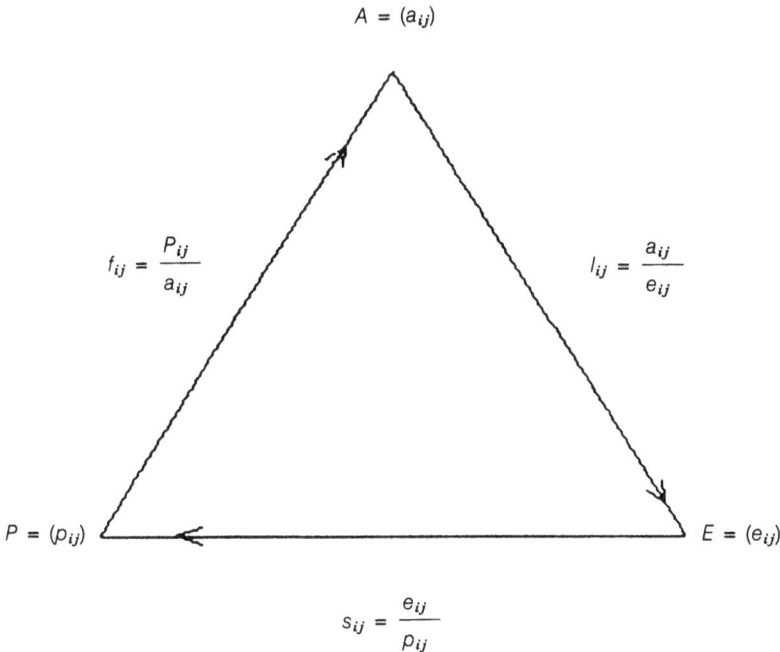

Figure 2. Comparisons of matrices of actual (*A*), perceived (*P*), and equitable (*E*) mobility and resulting measures of false consciousness (f_{ij}), feeling of injustice (s_{ij}), and illegitimacy (l_{ij}).[a]

[a]Arrows indicate the standard of comparison.

tor). If the value of the ratio is larger than 1, then the frequency compared is overestimated with respect to the standard. In practice, overestimated frequencies are compensated for by underestimated ones.

The ratios f_{ij}, s_{ij}, and l_{ij} characterize "local" discrepancies of the compared matrices with respect to their standards; they can be interpreted as "errors." The global measure of the discrepancy, based on the ratios, is given by the formula

$$L^2 = \Sigma x_{ij} \log(x_{ij}/y_{ij})$$

where x_{ij} denotes the compared frequencies and y_{ij} denotes the standard ones. The measure L^2 is the goodness of fit index, also known as the likelihood-ratio test statistic (Bishop et al., 1975:125). This index, used in the modelling approach to mobility tables, expresses a weighted sum of errors of prediction in which the frequencies of the compared matrix are the weights and the standard matrix is the model.

Since ratios f_{ij}, s_{ij}, and l_{ij} involve frequencies of mobility transitions, they are comparable; the values of L^2, as a global measure, can also be contrasted to allow for strict comparisons of P to A, E to P, and A to E. Thus, the differences in degrees of false consciousness, feeling of injustice, and illegitimacy can be investigated at both the local and global levels.

By comparing P to A we are able to assess the distortion of mobility perception—that is, the degree of false consciousness in the domain of social mobility. The ratio p_{ij}/a_{ij} resembles those used in psychophysical measurement, in which the intensity of psychological reaction is related as a ratio to the physical properties of the stimulus (for discussion of Fechner's and other psychological laws see Duncan, 1984).

In research on distributive justice, the sense of injustice is usually assessed by the discrepancy between the existing situation and an equitable one (e.g. Jasso, 1980; Phillips, 1983; Bell, 1974). Such conceptualization is theoretically grounded if perception of the existing situation is not distorted in the mind of the evaluator. However, social mobility is not perceived accurately, and therefore the feeling of injustice depends on the evaluator's perception of the reality rather than on the reality itself. Accordingly, the feeling of injustice in the domain of social mobility is conceptualized as a comparison of E to P. The feeling of injustice is diminished when equitable mobility closely corresponds to perceived mobility, and disappears when the two are equal.

By comparing matrix A to matrix E we assess the degree to which actual mobility is not legitimized, independently of how mobility is perceived. However, in our conceptualization, perceived mobility is indirectly involved in the definition of illegitimacy. Using the equality

$$f_{ij}s_{ij}l_{ij} = 1 \quad \text{(for all } i \text{ and } j\text{)}$$

we see that the measure l_{ij} can be expressed as

$$l_{ij} = (a_{ij}/p_{ij})(p_{ij}/e_{ij}).$$

Thus the extent of the illegitimacy of objective mobility is shown to be a function of the discrepancy between the existing situation (a_{ij}) from the perceived one (p_{ij}) and the discrepancy between the perceived state of affairs (p_{ij}) from the equitable one (e_{ij}).

Data

In this paper we study mobility patterns among the three major social classes in Poland: white-collar workers (the intelligentsia), blue-collar workers (the working class), and farmers (the peasantry). We neglect other social classes—such as the petite bourgeoisie or the lumpenproletariat—because their role in class structure has diminished in recent decades and is no longer important for the overall social mobility process (e.g. Zagórski, 1976). Moreover, the perception of upward and downward mobility is based on the trichotomous division involving the major social classes (Nowak, 1969; Janicka, 1976).

The data on actual social mobility were collected in 1982, in a study using a national sample of 1727 persons (Domański and Sawiński, 1984:120). The mobility table constructed on the basis of these data will be compared to identically constructed mobility tables containing perceived and normative frequencies.

Subjective data on social mobility were collected in 1982 from 280 students of the University of Warsaw. A questionnaire was administered to ten groups of students under the guidance of sociologists trained in research methods. Questions concerning social mobility were tested in a pilot study and the results obtained were used in modifying them. In particular, it was evident that students consider male and female mobility rates to be equal and are not aware of differences in fertility rates among social classes. For these reasons the final version of the questions pertained not strictly to men but to both sexes.

The perception of mobility frequencies was elicited by means of three questions. The first question was: "In your opinion, among one hundred randomly selected *blue-collar workers*, how many were brought up in the families of white-collar workers, blue-collar workers, and farmers?" The second and third questions respectively substituted "white-collar workers" and "farmers" for the (italicized above) category of blue-collar workers. To each group of student-respondents it was explained that the type of family origin was defined by the occupation of the head of the household. In addition, respondents were asked about the proportions of white-collar workers, blue-collar workers, and farmers in the labor force. Answers to the complete set of questions allow one to construct a table of perceived mobility for each respondent.

In order to obtain the normative mobility frequencies we asked the following question: "From among one hundred children of blue-collar workers, how many should grow up to become white-collar workers, blue-collar workers, and farmers in order to achieve social justice?" In the two subsequent questions, "white-collar workers" and "farmers" were substituted for the reference category of blue-collar workers. Having answered these questions, the respondents were asked to fill in a table by providing percentages of outflow distributions for each class of origin. Since the pilot study showed that students are not aware of the differences in fertility among social classes, we were justified in using the perceived distribution of adults in three classes as a basis for contructing the table of equitable mobility frequencies.

The first panel of Table 1 contains frequencies of the actual mobility of employed men aged 19 to 65; the second and third panels display average frequencies of the perceived and equitable mobility of a population assumed to be closely comparable. Average frequencies were obtained from the limited sample of student-respondents. The variability of responses was analyzed with re-

Table 1

Frequencies of Actual, Perceived, and Equitable Mobility, with Totals Standardized to 1,000

Origin \ Destination	White-collar	Blue-collar	Farmers	Total
(1) Actual mobility				
White-collar	80	55	4	139
Blue-collar	89	283	23	395
Farmers	60	209	197	466
Total	229	547	224	1,000
(2) Perceived mobility				
White-collar	189	60	15	264
Blue-collar	96	254	25	375
Farmers	46	147	168	361
Total	331	461	208	1,000
(3) Equitable mobility				
White-collar	201	89	40	331
Blue-collar	134	272	55	461
Farmers	33	50	125	208
Total	369	411	220	1,000

spect to two characteristics: class origin and major subject studied. Small intergroup differences justified the aggregation of all responses.

Three matrices presented in Table 1 differ from each other to a great extent; however, a large part of this difference occurs because of the intermatrix discrepancy between origin and destination distributions. This discrepancy should be eliminated before comparing various kinds of mobility in terms of their mobility regimes (Hauser, 1978; 1979).

Analysis and results

The initial step in the comparison of perceived to actual mobility, equitable to perceived mobility, and actual to equitable mobility

Table 2

Frequencies of Perceived Mobility Adjusted to Row and Column Sums of Actual Mobility

Origin \ Destination	White-collar	Blue-collar	Farmers	Total
White-collar	93	39	7	139
Blue-collar	84	289	22	395
Farmers	57	219	195	460
Total	229	547	224	1,000

consists in adjusting the margins of the compared mobility matrix to the margins of its standard. We achieved this adjustment by means of the well known Deming-Stephan iterative algorithm (Deming and Stephan, 1940; Deming, 1943). The algorithm leaves invariant the mobility regime in the sense of preserving odds ratios of mobility frequencies. Thus the adjusted frequencies of the compared matrix represent its original mobility regime, net of the intermatrix discrepancy of the margins. Table 2 provides an example of the matrix of mobility frequencies after margins adjustment.

The reasons for margin adjustment in pairwise comparisons of matrices—P to A, E to P, and A to E—are straightforward. In the comparison of perceived mobility to actual mobility it is natural to abstract from distortion in the perceived distributions of origin and destination. In order to eliminate the effects of equitable origin and destination distributions on mobility frequencies, we replaced these distributions by those of perceived mobility. Finally, in comparing actual mobility to equitable mobility we obtain the frequencies of the former that would occur under equitable distributions of origins and destinations.

Table 3 characterizes local and global discrepancies between matrices for each compared pair. Although the extreme value of overestimation is contained in the matrix describing false consciousness, the overall distortion of the perceived mobility regime is relatively small. We argue that actual mobility is per-

Table 3

Ratios of Mobility Frequencies Expressing the Measures of False Consciousness (f_{ij}), Feeling of Injustice (s_{ij}), and Illegitimacy (l_{ij})

Origin	Destination	White-collar	Blue collar	Farmers
(1) Ratios f_{ij} of perceived mobility frequencies to actual mobility frequencies[a]				
($L^2 = 5.5$)				
White-collar		1.16	.71	1.75
Blue-collar		.94	1.02	.96
Farmers		.87	1.05	.99
(2) Ratios s_{ij} of equitable mobility frequencies to perceived mobility frequencies[a]				
($L^2 = 15.8$)				
White-collar		.85	1.42	1.27
Blue-collar		1.05	.98	1.04
Farmers		1.52	.87	.97
(3) Ratios l_{ij} of actual mobility frequencies to equitable mobility frequencies[a]				
($L^2 = 11.2$)				
White-collar		1.07	1.07	.50
Blue-collar		.98	.98	1.15
Farmers		.67	.98	1.10

[a]Frequencies of compared matrix divided by corresponding frequencies of standard matrix. Prior to the division the compared matrix was adjusted to the row sums and column sums of the standard matrix.

ceived rather accurately. If the respondents do not take into account any association between origins and destinations—that is, if their perception of mobility approximates random assignment—then the resulting perceived mobility would differ greatly from the actual one ($L^2 = 168.1$). Treating the random assignment as the baseline, we observe that the perceived mobility, net of marginal effects, fits reality extremely well ($L^2 = 5.5$), accounting for 97 percent of association.

University students perceive much less mobility from farmers to white-collar workers than actually occurs: this is shown in Tables 1 and 3. Net of marginal effects, students consider as equitable much more mobility (farmers to–white-collar workers) than they perceive. In consequence, the actual mobility from farmers to white-collar workers is not legitimized by the respondents; the amount of this kind of mobility is much smaller than that required by their equity standard.

In contrast, for both perceived and equitable mobility, students overestimate the amount of mobility from white-collar workers to farmers; this is reflected in the magnitude and direction of the measures of false consciousness and feeling of injustice. However, the actual mobility from white-collar workers to farmers is still too low to be legitimized.

These examples show how the ratios of compared mobility frequencies to standard ones can be analyzed. We should note, however, that because of margin adjustments the equality $f_{ij} s_{ij} l_{ij} = 1$ is only approximated. However, adjustment of margins of perceived and equitable mobility to margins of actual mobility does not change the qualitative conclusions. Even under these common margins for all matrices the main conclusion still remains valid: the degree of false consciousness is smaller than the degree of illegitimacy, and both are smaller than the degree of the feeling of injustice. That students sense more injustice than actually exists according to their own equity standards was an unexpected finding.

Summary

From the theoretical standpoint, this paper attempts to integrate the objective, cognitive and normative dimensions of social mobility. This integration is based on a comparison of the matrices of actual, perceived and equitable frequencies of transitions between origins and destinations. The ratios of compared frequencies operationally define the degree of false consciousness, feeling of injustice and illegitimacy in the domain of social mobility.

From the methodological standpoint we propose a practical method for ascertaining cognitive and normative mobility frequencies. In this paper we used average frequencies for the entire sample, although an analysis of individual images and preferences of mobility frequencies can be performed. This extension would seem particularly useful for heterogeneous samples with respect to the social positions of the respondents.

From the empirical standpoint we have demonstrated that, net of marginal effects, the matrices of actual, perceived and equitable mobility do not differ very much from each other, at least in terms of the goodness of fit. Within a small range of differences the measure of false consciousness has a smaller value than the measure of illegitimacy, which is still smaller than the measure of the feeling of injustice.

References

Bell, W.
    1974   "A conceptual analysis of equality and equity in evolutionary perspective." *American Behavioral Scientist* 18 (No. 1):8-35.

Bishop, Y.M.M., S.E. Fienberg, and P.W. Holland
    1975   *Discrete Multivariate Analysis: Theory and Practice*. Cambridge, Mass.: M.I.T. Press.

Della Fave, L.R.
    1980   "The meek shall not inherit the earth: self-evaluation and legitimacy of stratification." *American Sociological Review* 45:955-71.

Deming, W.E.
    1943   *Statistical Adjustment of Data*. New York: Wiley.

Deming, W.E. and F. Stephan
    1940   "On a least squares adjustment of a sample frequency table when the expected marginal totals are known." *Annals of Mathematical Statistics* 11:427-44.

Domański, H. and Z. Sawiński
    1984   "Prestiż i pozycja społeczna jako wymiary ruchliwości zawodowej." [Prestige and social position as dimensions of occupational mobility.] *Studia Socjologiczne* No. 2 (93):107-25.

Duncan, O.D.
    1984   Notes on Social Measurement. New York: Russell-Sage.

Featherman, D.L.
    1981   "Social stratification and mobility: two decades of cumulative social science." *American Behavioral Scientist* 24:364-85.

Goldthorpe, J.H. (in collaboration with C. Llewellyn and C. Payne)
    1980   *Social Mobility and Class Structure in Modern Britain.* Oxford: Clarendon Press.

Harrop, M.
    1980   "Popular conceptions of mobility." *Sociology* 14:89-98.

Hauser, R.M.
    1978   "A structural model of the mobility table." *Social Forces* 56:919-53.
    1979   "Some explanatory methods for modeling mobility tables and other cross-classified data." Pp. 413-58 in K.F. Schuessler (ed.), *Sociological Methodology*, 1980. San Francisco: Jossey-Bass.

Janicka, K.
    1976   *Ruchliwość międzypokoleniowa i jej korelaty.* [Intergenerational Mobility and Its Correlates.] Wrocław: Ossolineum.

Jasso, G.
    1980   "A new theory of distributive justice." *American Sociological Review* 45:3-32.

Kerckhoff, A.C.
    1984   "The current state of social mobility research." *Sociological Quarterly* 25 (Spring):139-53.

Mach, B.W., K.M. Słomczyński, and W. Wesołowski
    1978   "Introduction: Some trends in the sociology of social mobility." Pp. 7-34 in W. Wesołowski, K.M. Słomczyński, and B.W. Mach (eds.), *Social Mobility in Comparative Perspective.* Wrocław: Ossolineum.

Mach, B.W. and W. Wesołowski
    1982   *Ruchliwość a teoria struktury społecznej.* [Mobility and the Theory of Social Structure.] Warsaw: Polish Scientific Publishers.

Matras, J.
    1980   "Comparative social mobility." *Annual Review of Sociology* 6:401-31.

Mayer, K.U.
    1979   "Class formation and social reproduction." Pp. 37-56 in J. Berting, F. Geyer and R. Jurkovich (eds.) *Problems in International Comparative Research in the Social Sciences.* Oxford: Pergamon Press.

Narojek, W.
    1982   *Struktura społeczna w doświadczeniu jednostki.* [Social Structure in the Individual's Experience.] Warsaw: State Publishing House.

Nowak, S.
    1969   "Changes in social structure in social consciousness." Pp. 235-247 in C.S. Heller (ed.), *Structured Social Inequality.* New York: Macmillan.

Phillips, D.
    1983   "The normative standing of economic inequalities." *Sociologische Gids* 30 (September):318-50.

Simkus, A.
　1981　"Comparative stratification and mobility." *International Journal of Comparative Sociology* 22:213-36.
Zagórski, K.
　1976　*Zmiany struktury i ruchliwość społeczno-zawodowa w Polsce.* [Changes of Structure and Socio-occupational Mobility in Poland.] Warsaw: Central Statistical Office.

About the Editors

KAZIMIERZ M. SŁOMCZYŃSKI is an Associate Professor at the Institute of Sociology, University of Warsaw, Poland. From 1978 through 1985 he was a Visiting Scientist at the Laboratory of Socio-environmental Studies, National Institute of Mental Health, and he is currently Visiting Associate Professor of Sociology at the Johns Hopkins University. Dr. Słomczyński is the author or editor of 13 books on the subject of social stratification. TADEUSZ K. KRAUZE is Professor and Chair of the Department of Sociology and Anthropology at Hofstra University in Hempstead, New York. He is the author of numerous articles on social stratification and on the sociology of science. Together SŁOMCZYŃSKI and KRAUZE edited *Class Structure and Social Mobility in Poland* (M.E. Sharpe, 1978).

For Product Safety Concerns and Information please contact our EU representative GPSR@taylorandfrancis.com
Taylor & Francis Verlag GmbH, Kaufingerstraße 24, 80331 München, Germany

www.ingramcontent.com/pod-product-compliance
Lightning Source LLC
Chambersburg PA
CBHW070610300426

44113CB00010B/1483